Intro

After the Oklahoma City bombing, _____ to quit working as a copier technician to stay at home with the kids. Since I have a hard time sitting still and had always wanted to be a bakery chef, I decided to take a cake decorating course. It seems as if that is what God wanted me to do, because all of a sudden I had a talent for decorating. With the decorating, I loved experimenting with recipes. All of my cakes were made scratch and, over time; I developed my own recipes, for which I have won some awards.

A few years later, with my husband's job change, we moved to the country. This put quite a crimp on cake orders, so I opened a shop called "The Sugar Fix". Here I made all kinds of cakes, cookies, bars, soups, and sandwiches. It was wonderful for people to come in who would refuse to eat a particular dessert or soup, try mine, and then order large quantities of their new favorite. Quality and freshness were my main goals. I used the best ingredients I could find. A lot of searching helped me to find the best without necessarily buying the most expensive.

Sadly, after 8 months of doing quite well, I became ill and had to close the shop. A few months later I was diagnosed with Multiple Sclerosis. My wonderful customers still check on me from time to time and have asked when I plan to publish a cookbook. So, after a few years of adjusting to the shock of the illness, I decided to really get to work on it. This book is a tribute to "The Sugar Fix", my husband, two boys, parents, friends, and customers. I hope everyone enjoys these recipes as much as I enjoyed developing them.

Some of the best things to eat are the easiest. I do my best to make recipes that are amazing, but not difficult. Some are a little more time consuming than others, but worth the time. Many of my recipes can be ready to eat in less than an hour. I have also included some tips to make things move along more quickly and easily. The book contains mostly desserts because that is my passion; however, I have included some dinner recipes that really blew my family and customers away.

THE SUGAR FIX

The recipes and rantings of an obsessive-compulsive cook

By

Michele Foster

© 2004 Michele Foster.
All Rights Reserved.

No part of this book may be reproduced, stored in a retrieval system, or transmitted by any means without the written permission of the author.

ISBN: 1-4140-5627-3 (e)
ISBN: 1-4140-5626-5 (sc)

Library of Congress Control Number: 2004090213
Printed in the United States of America
Bloomington, Indiana

This book is printed on acid-free paper.

1st Books - rev. 06/28/04

Table of Contents

TIPS & TRICKS ix

CAKES 1
   Almond Cake 3
   The BEST Chocolate Cake 4
   Spiced Pound Cake 6
   Cherry Cake 7
   Spiced-Up Cake 8
   Angel Food Cake 9
   Orange Spice Bundt Cake 10
   Carrot Cake 11
   Almond Pound Cake 13
   Elegant White Cake 15
   Ginger Chocolate Cake 16
   Coconut Cream Cake 17
   Lemonade Cake 18
   Mississippi Mud Cake 19
   Chocolate Glaze 19
   Orange Cake 20
   Chocolate Sheet Cake 21
   Strawberry Cake 22
   Pineapple Upside-Down Cake 24
   Buttermilk Pound Cake 25
   Chocolate Chip Cake 27
   Lemon Pound Cake 28
   Applesauce Cake 29

FROSTINGS 31
   White Buttercream Frosting 32
   White Chocolate Buttercream Frosting 32
   Lemon Buttercream Frosting 34
   Chocolate Buttercream Frosting 34
   Chocolate Amaretto Buttercream Frosting 35
   Double Fudge Buttercream Frosting 35

Ginger Hint Fudge Frosting 36
Chocolate Sheet Cake Frosting 36
Old Fashioned Frosting 37
Cream Cheese Frosting 37
Spiced Cream Cheese Frosting 38
Coconut Cake Cream Frosting 38
Vanilla Fondant 39
White Chocolate Fondant 40
Chocolate Fondant 42
Ginger Chocolate Fondant 44
Lemon Fondant 45
Italian Buttercream 47
Chocolate Italian Buttercream 48
Sweetened Whipped Cream 48
Vanilla Glaze 49
Lemon Glaze 49
Rum Glaze 49
Chocolate Glaze 50
Chocolate Amaretto Glaze 50
Royal Icing 51

PIES 53
   Apple Pie Filling 54
   Pecan Pie 55
   Cherry Pie Filling 56
   Vanilla Cream Pie 57
   Lemon Pie 58
   Chocolate Cream Pie 59
   Italian Meringue 60
   Quick & Easy Lemon Pie 61
   Key Lime Pie 62
   Caramel Pie Filling 63
   Basic Pie Crust 64
   Cookie Crust 65
   Graham Cracker Crust 65
   Chocolate Cookie Crust 66
   Coconut/Cookie Crust 66

DESSERTS ... 67
    Baked Fudge ... 68
    Piña Colada Cheesecake ... 69
    Topping ... 70
    Lemon Bars ... 71
    Marshmallow Whirl Brownies ... 72
    Ginger Crunch Bars ... 73
    Pecan Crunch Bars ... 74
    Caramel Sauce ... 75
    Cheesecake ... 76
    Caramel Pecan Cheesecake ... 77
    Chocolate Earthquake ... 78
    Apple Crisp ... 79
    Creamy Chocolate Torte ... 80
    Chocolate Sauce ... 80
    Orange Rum Glaze ... 81
    Glossy Chocolate Sauce ... 81
    Lemon Sauce ... 82

COOKIES ... 83
    Snickerdoodles ... 84
    Chocolate Chip Cookies ... 85
    Desert Cookies ... 86
    Chocolate Peanut Butter Chip Cookies ... 87
    Oatmeal Cookies ... 88
    Crispy Crunchy Chocolate Chip Cookies ... 89
    Sugar Cookies ... 90
    Triple Chippers ... 91
    Cut Out Cookie Dough ... 92
    Brown Sugar Cut Out Cookies ... 94
    Chocolate Cut Out Cookies ... 95
    Gooey Bars ... 96
    Peanut Butter Cookies ... 97
    Peanut Butter Chocolate Chip Cookies ... 97

A MESSAGE FROM THE AUTHOR. ... 98

DINNERS 99
- Chicken & Dumplings 100
- Beef Stew 101
- Tortilla Soup 102
- Italian Sausage Stew 103
- Garlic Chicken & Rice 104
- Perfectly Easy Roast 105
- Gravy 105
- Garlic Chicken Soup 106
- Lasagna 107
- Sausage Bread 108
- Taco Pie 109
- Chicken & Rice 110
- Onion Burgers 111
- No Effort BBQ 112

MISCELLANEOUS RECIPES 113
- Pan Coating 114
- Banana Nut Bread 115
- Buttermilk Biscuits 116
- Ice Box Rolls 117
- Pumpkin Bread 118
- Bread Machine Bread 119
- Light Wheat 119
- Gumpaste 121
- Gum Glue 123
- Pastillage 124
- Chocolate Leather 126

Tips & Tricks

- **Read recipe thoroughly before starting.**
- When cracking eggs, always break into a separate measuring cup to be sure eggs are good and for the easier removal of any shell that might end up falling into the cup.
- Always pre-heat the oven to the stated temperature. This prevents improper cooking or possibly burning during the cooking process.
- Start the oven before mixing any ingredients.
- All ingredients should be room temperature. This provides for better mixing and rising results.
- To warm eggs quickly, place them in a bowl with very warm water for about 5 minutes.
- Unsalted butter is preferred, but margarine can be used. Cakes and cookies will have a slightly different texture and flavor.
- Low fat spreads should <u>not</u> be used in these recipes.
- Be sure that your oven is level and is baking at the proper temperature.
- For cakes with no center hump, try pan wraps soaked in water. These are available at craft stores and bakery supply stores.
- Have all ingredients ready before beginning the recipe, then put each away as it is used. This ensures that nothing is left out of the recipe.
- Toast nuts in $350°$ oven for about 15 minutes for the best flavor. When nuts are hot to the touch, they are done. Allow the nuts to cool completely then store in a plastic zipper bag in the freezer.
- A large strainer makes a great sifter.
- Scoop dry ingredients into the measuring cup, then level with edge of scoop for accurate measuring.
- Do not use a liquid measuring cup for dry ingredients.
- Do not shake dry ingredients to level. This compacts the ingredients and can adversely affect the recipe.
- Lightly stir dry ingredients to "lighten" them.
- For freezing cakes, wrap the cake with plastic wrap three times, sealing each layer. Place the cake in the freezer, when frozen, wrap with two layers of aluminum foil or one layer of heavy-duty foil. For thawing, allow the cake to come to room temperature before removing any wrapping.

Cakes

Almond Cake	3
The BEST Chocolate Cake	4
Spiced Pound Cake	6
Cherry Cake	7
Spiced-Up Cake	8
Angel Food Cake	9
Orange Spice Bundt Cake	10
Carrot Cake	11
Almond Pound Cake	13
Elegant White Cake	15
Ginger Chocolate Cake	16
Coconut Cream Cake	17
Lemonade Cake	18
Mississippi Mud Cake	19
Chocolate Glaze	19
Orange Cake	20
Chocolate Sheet Cake	21
Strawberry Cake	22
Pineapple Upside-Down Cake	24
Buttermilk Pound Cake	25
Chocolate Chip Cake	27
Lemon Pound Cake	28
Applesauce Cake	29

The Secret Garden

This cake is an emerald green with white "gumpaste" or sugar chrysanthemums, white freesias, and green and white hosta leaves. The lace to the right of the flowers is hand painted gold stringwork, also known as extension work. It only touches the cake at the top of the strings. The stand is black with gold trim and was made specifically for this cake. It received a gold certificate at the Oklahoma State Sugar Art Show in 2003.

Cakes

The mellow taste of almonds is a nice change from the traditional white cake. Chocolate or White Chocolate Frosting goes quite well with it.

Almond Cake

350°   35 minutes

3 cups cake flour
1 ½ cups sugar
1 Tbsp. baking powder
½ tsp. baking soda
½ tsp. salt
1 cup butter, softened
1 ¼ cup buttermilk
2 eggs
2 tsp. real vanilla
1 tsp. almond extract

Sift together flour, sugar, baking powder, baking soda, and salt. Add butter and 1 cup of the buttermilk. Mix slowly until combined then beat at medium speed for 90 seconds. Meanwhile, mix eggs and vanilla with remaining buttermilk. Scrape down sides. Add to batter; mixing in two batches for about 20 seconds each. Pour into 2 - 8" or one 9"x13" prepared pan(s). Bake at 350° for 35 minutes. Allow cakes to cool for 10 minutes before turning out onto cooling racks. Allow cakes to cool completely before frosting. Frost with White Buttercream Frosting or White Chocolate Frosting (page 34).

Although pure extracts are more expensive, they will make a world of difference in the taste of your cakes and frostings.

THE SUGAR FIX

I love this cake almost as much as my family. It's perfect with or without frosting. For cake decorator's, this cake carves beautifully for sculptured cakes. Always "crumb coat" the cake before putting on the finishing frosting. Crumb coating is a very thin layer of frosting to keep the crumbs from mixing with the frosting. Let it stand for about 10 minutes before continuing to decorate. I have won several blue ribbons for this cake with the Double Fudge Frosting, page 37.

The BEST Chocolate Cake

325^0 45 minutes

1 cup butter, softened
5 Tbsp. Jersey cocoa
2 cups sugar
2 eggs
2 tsp. vanilla
½ tsp. almond extract
3 cups cake flour
2 tsp. baking soda
½ tsp. salt
1 cup buttermilk
1 cup boiling water

Cream the butter, cocoa, and sugar until light and fluffy. Add eggs, one at a time. Add almond extract and vanilla; mix well. Sift together flour, baking soda, and salt. Add alternately with buttermilk, beginning and ending with flour. Slowly add boiling water. Mix well. <u>BATTER WILL BE THIN. DO NOT ADD FLOUR</u>. Pour into 2-8" & 1 6" prepared round pans (to prevent overflow) or one 9"x13" pan. Bake for 45 minutes. Cool 10 minutes before cooling on rack. When cool, frost with Chocolate Frosting or White Chocolate Frosting (page 34).

Mocha Chocolate Cake

Substitute 1 cup very hot, strong coffee for boiling water.

Cinnamon Chocolate Cake

Substitute 1 tsp. cinnamon for almond extract.

Cakes

Roaring Twenties

All of the instruments are handmade with gumpaste, the pictures are hand painted with liquid food coloring, and all the panels are hand cut fondant.

THE SUGAR FIX

This is a really moist and delicious change of pace for a pound cake. The Orange Rum Glaze and Glossy Chocolate Sauce are wonderful complements to this cake.

Spiced Pound Cake

325°   1 hour 15 minutes

1 ½ cup butter, softened
1 ½ cups brown sugar
1 cup sugar
3 eggs
2 tsp. vanilla
1 tsp. Cinnamon
½ tsp. Allspice
½ tsp. Cloves
¼ tsp. ginger
3 ½ cups cake flour
¼ tsp. baking soda
1 tsp. salt
1 cup buttermilk
½ cup chopped pecans

Cream the butter and sugars, beating until fluffy. Add eggs, one at a time, beating well after each. Add vanilla, cinnamon, allspice, cloves, and ginger. Sift together flour, baking soda, and salt. Add alternately with buttermilk, beginning and ending with flour. Pour into prepared Bundt pan with pecans sprinkled into the bottom and bake for 1 hour 15 minutes. Cool 15 minutes, and then turn out onto wire rack to cool completely.

This cake won first place at the Oklahoma State Sugar Art Show Tasting Division in Tulsa, Oklahoma, October 2003. The sauce and glaze were big hits with the judges.

White chocolate frosting is the perfect accompaniment for this cake. It's also a beautiful pink cake that is moist and delicious.

Cherry Cake

350⁰   35 minutes

*3 cups cake flour
1 ½ cups sugar
1 Tbsp. baking powder
½ tsp. baking soda
½ tsp. salt
2 Tbsp. cherry gelatin
1 cup butter, softened
1 ¼ cups buttermilk
2 eggs
2 tsp. real vanilla
1 tsp. cherry flavoring
½ tsp. almond extract*

Sift together flour, sugar, baking powder, baking soda, salt, and orange gelatin powder. Add butter and 1 cup of the buttermilk. Mix slowly until combined then beat at medium speed for 90 seconds. Meanwhile, mix eggs, vanilla, almond extract, and cherry flavoring with remaining buttermilk. Scrape down sides. Add to batter; mixing in two batches for about 20 seconds each. Pour into 2 - 8" or one 9"x13" prepared pan(s). Bake at 350⁰ for 35 minutes. Allow cakes to cool for 10 minutes before turning out onto cooling racks. Allow cakes to cool completely before frosting.

THE SUGAR FIX

I love spice cake, but most are dry and tasteless. I played with this recipe until I got it just right. The Spiced Cream Cheese Frosting is phenomenal on this cake. If you like nuts, stir ½ cup toasted pecans or walnuts into batter and sprinkle some on top.

Spiced-Up Cake

350°   *35 minutes*

*3 cups sifted cake flour
1 ¼ cups sugar
1 cup brown sugar
1 tsp. salt
1 tsp. baking powder
1 tsp. baking soda
1 tsp. cinnamon
1 tsp. cloves
1 tsp. allspice
½ tsp. ginger
1 cup butter, softened
1 ¼ cups buttermilk
3 eggs
2 tsp. vanilla*

In large mixer bowl, combine all dry ingredients. Add 1 cup of the buttermilk and butter. Mix slowly then beat at medium speed (high speed if using hand mixer) for 90 seconds. Meanwhile, add eggs and vanilla to remaining buttermilk. Scrape down sides of bowl; then add egg mixture to batter in two batches, mixing approximately 20 seconds after each addition. Pour into two 9" round prepared pans. Bake at 350° for 40 minutes or until toothpick is inserted and comes out clean. Cool in pan for 10 minutes, then on wire rack until cool. Frost with Spiced Cream Cheese Frosting or White Chocolate Frosting (pages 40 & 39).

When I have done bridal shows, I have a friend that <u>insists</u> that this be one of the cakes that I bring for samples. It usually goes as quickly as the chocolate.

Cakes

I love Angel Food Cake, but don't like the taste of egg whites, so a little vanilla bean paste* and some almond extract make this cake delicious. If vanilla bean paste is not available, substitute 2 teaspoons real vanilla. Sliced strawberries and freshly made whipped cream are wonderful on this cake.

Angel Food Cake

350° 40 min.

1 ½ cups egg whites
1 tsp. cream of tartar
1 tsp. vanilla bean paste*
½ tsp. almond extract
1 cup superfine sugar
1 ½ cups powdered sugar, sifted
1 cup cake flour, sifted
½ tsp. salt

In large stand mixer bowl beat at medium speed egg whites and cream of tartar to soft peaks. Add vanilla bean paste and almond extract; then gradually add superfine sugar. Continue to beat at medium until stiff, but not dry, peaks form. While egg whites are beating, sift dry ingredients three times. When egg whites are ready, sift about ¼ of the flour mixture over whites; fold in gently. Repeat until flour is incorporated. Pour into lightly oiled 10" tube pan. Bake on lowest rack for 40 minutes. Invert cake in pan; cool completely. Loosen with very thin, flexible spatula; remove from pan.

*Vanilla bean paste can be found at specialty stores.

Go against convention by <u>lightly</u> oiling the pan. It does not cause the cake to go flat and it is much easier to remove.

THE SUGAR FIX

Another experiment! Although this is not the recipe I used for the competition in 2003, it was a contender in the "at home" competition.

Orange Spice Bundt Cake

325°   1 hour 15 min.

1 cup butter
1 cup sugar
1 ½ cups brown sugar
3 eggs
2 tsp. vanilla
1 tsp. cinnamon
¼ tsp. allspice
¼ tsp. cloves
¼ tsp. ginger
3 ½ cups cake flour
1 tsp. salt
¼ tsp. baking soda
¾ cup buttermilk
¼ cup freshly squeezed orange juice
½ tsp. orange zest
¼ cup toasted pecans, coarsely chopped (optional)
¼ cup butter, melted (optional)

Cream butter and sugars; beat until light and fluffy. Add eggs, once at a time, mixing well after each. Add vanilla and spices. Sift together flour, salt, and baking soda. Add alternately with flour, mixing well after each. Add orange juice and zest; beat until just combined. If desired, pour ½ cup melted butter into prepared Bundt pan and sprinkle with chopped pecan. Bake for 1 hour 15 minutes or until wooden skewer comes out clean. Allow to cool 15 minutes before turning out onto cake plate; cool completely. Top with chocolate sauce or an orange glaze.

Cakes

Baby carrots are my choice for this cake. Not only are they less bitter, but they don't need to be peeled or chopped. I'm all for less effort!

Carrot Cake

325^0 40-45 minutes

3 ½ cups flour
2 cups sugar
1 ½ tsp. baking powder
1 tsp. baking soda
1 tsp. salt
1 tsp. cinnamon
½ tsp. cloves
¼ tsp. ginger
½ tsp. allspice
½ cup peanut oil*
3 eggs
2 tsp. vanilla
½ cup buttermilk
3 cups shredded carrots

Combine dry ingredients. Mix together oil, eggs, vanilla, and buttermilk. Add to dry mixture. Mix well by hand. Stir in carrots. Pour into two 8" pans lined with waxed paper and prepared with pan coating. Bake at 325^0 for 40 to 45 minutes. Remove from oven when toothpick comes out clean. Allow cakes to cool for 10 minutes then turn out onto cooling rack. Allow cakes to cool completely before frosting cake. Frost with Cream Cheese Frosting or Spiced Cream Cheese Frosting for something really special (pages 39 & 40).

<u>*For those with peanut allergies, substitute cooled, melted butter.</u>

Use a food processor to grate carrots. Remember to remove any large pieces.

THE SUGAR FIX

Happy Birthday Scooter

The dog in this cake was modeled after our beagle, Rocky. However, it was named Scooter for a friend of mine who had had a dog named Scooter. The butterfly, hat, shingles, and all the decorations are either gumpaste or royal icing. The "wood" is made with fondant and a rubber stamp was used to make the wood grain.

Cakes

This very moist cake is perfect for holidays, picnics, or a gift dessert for a dinner party. It's very rich, so a little goes a long way.

Almond Pound Cake

350°   1 hour, 15 min.

½ cup almond paste
1 cup butter, softened
1 ¼ cups sugar
4 eggs
2 ½ cups cake flour
1 tsp. baking powder
½ tsp. salt
½ cup buttermilk
2 tsp. vanilla
½ tsp. almond extract

Beat almond paste and butter until smooth. Add sugar; beat until fluffy. Add eggs, one at a time, beating well after each. Sift together flour, baking powder, and salt. Add alternately with buttermilk, beginning and ending with flour; mix until smooth. Add vanilla and almond extract; mix well. Pour into prepared Bundt pan; bake until skewer inserted comes out clean. Cool 30 minutes, then turn out on serving plate. Frost with glaze, page 34, while still warm, not hot.

THE SUGAR FIX

Antique Inspiration

An antique water pitcher inspired this cake. The roses are pink, the daisies are blue, and the leaves are a medium green. The "lace" is white three tiered stringwork with lace points and embroidery to embellish the design.
I received Best of Show at the 2003 Oklahoma State Sugar Art Show, and First place at the Texas Sugar Art Show.

Cakes

A lot of time and effort went into the experiments to make this recipe. It is so flavorful that it tastes great with or without frosting. It's very easy to make and with a little practice, it can be in the oven in less than 10 minutes. Just about any frosting can be used for a very special wedding or birthday cake.

Elegant White Cake

350⁰   *35 minutes*

3 cups cake flour
1 ½ cups sugar
1 Tbsp. baking powder
½ tsp. baking soda
½ tsp. salt
1 cup butter, softened
1 ¼ cup buttermilk
2 eggs
2 tsp. real vanilla

Sift together flour, sugar, baking powder, baking soda, and salt. Add butter and 1 cup of the buttermilk. Mix slowly until combined then beat at medium speed for 90 seconds. Meanwhile, mix eggs and vanilla with remaining buttermilk. Scrape down sides. Add to batter; mixing in two batches for about 20 seconds each. Pour into 2 - 8" or one 9"x13" prepared pan(s). Bake at 350⁰ for 35 minutes. Allow cakes to cool for 10 minutes before turning out onto cooling racks. Allow cakes to cool completely before frosting.

THE SUGAR FIX

I love to enter competitions and one in particular requires the use of ginger, chocolate, and vanilla. It's not as easy as it sounds!

Ginger Chocolate Cake

325^0 45 minutes

1 cup butter, softened
5 Tbsp. cocoa
2 cups sugar
2 eggs
1 tsp. ginger
2 tsp. vanilla extract
3 cups cake flour
2 tsp. baking soda
½ tsp. salt
1 cup buttermilk
1 cup boiling water

Cream butter, cocoa, and sugar until light and fluffy. Add eggs, one at a time. Add ginger and vanilla; mix well. Sift together flour, baking soda, and salt. Add alternately with buttermilk, beginning and ending with flour. Slowly add boiling water. Mix well. BATTER WILL BE THIN. DO NOT ADD FLOUR. Pour into 2-8" & 1 6" round pans (to prevent overflow). Bake for 45 minutes. Cool 10 minutes before cooling on rack.

My mom loves this cake and usually requests it for her birthday. It's very rich and somewhat time consuming to make. This cake is very pretty for holiday gatherings or to bring for a special dinner party with friends.

Coconut Cream Cake

350°   30-35 minutes

1 cup butter, softened
2 cups sugar
2 tsp. vanilla
5 eggs, separated
2 cups sifted cake flour
1 tsp. baking soda
1 cup buttermilk
½ tsp. salt
1 cup flaked coconut

Cream butter, sugar, and vanilla on medium speed until light and fluffy. Add egg yolks, one at a time, mixing well after each. Sift together flour, baking soda, and salt. Add alternately with buttermilk, beginning and ending with flour. Stir in coconut. Beat egg whites until stiff, but not dry; fold gently into batter. Pour into 3 – 9" round prepared pans. Bake at 350F for 30-35 minutes. Cool 10 minutes, then turn out onto wire rack, cool completely. Frost and fill with Coconut Cake Cream Filling (page 40).

Toasted coconut will add a little color and different flavor for the adventurous.

THE SUGAR FIX

*Lemon cakes can sometime be over-powering and bitter. This cake is luscious with a very lemony frosting. I won a first place ribbon with this cake at the State Fair and got to do a little advertising on the local news for **"The Sugar Fix"** about a week before the grand opening.*

Lemonade Cake

350⁰   *35 minutes*

3 cups cake flour
1 ½ cups sugar
1 Tbsp. baking powder
½ tsp. baking soda
½ tsp. salt
1 small pkg. lemon pudding mix
1 cup butter, softened
1 ¼ cup buttermilk
2 eggs
2 tsp. vanilla extract
1 tsp. lemon extract

Sift together flour, sugar, baking powder, baking soda, salt, and lemon pudding mix. Add butter and 1 cup of the buttermilk. Mix slowly until combined then beat at medium speed for 90 seconds. Meanwhile, mix eggs, vanilla, and lemon extract with remaining buttermilk. After scraping down the sides of the bowl, add egg mixture to batter, mixing in two batches for about 20 seconds each. Pour into 2 - 8" or 9" prepared pans. Bake at 350⁰ for 35 minutes. Allow cakes to cool for 10 minutes before turning out onto cooling racks. Allow cakes to cool completely before frosting.

Cakes

When I was in high school, my favorite English teacher wanted this cake for her birthday every year. We weren't supposed to have parties at school, but I always took a couple of pieces to the administrators who were against parties. With cake in their hands, they didn't mind us having a party.

Mississippi Mud Cake

1 cup butter
2 cups sugar
¼ cup cocoa
4 eggs
½ tsp. salt
2 tsp. vanilla
1 ½ cups flour
1 cup pecans, toasted, chopped
1 cup coconut, toasted (opt.)
1 small jar marshmallow cream

Cream butter, sugar, and cocoa. Add eggs, salt, and vanilla. Stir in flour, pecans, and coconut (if used). Pour into prepared 9x13" pan. Bake at 350F for 30 minutes. Spread marshmallow cream over hot cake. Allow to cool completely, then ice with chocolate glaze.

Chocolate Glaze

½ cup butter
½ cup evaporated milk
2 tsp. vanilla
½ tsp. salt
4 cups powdered sugar, sifted
½ cup cocoa, sifted

Beat butter, evaporated milk, vanilla, and salt until smooth. Add powdered sugar and cocoa slowly; mix until smooth. Pour over cooled cake.

THE SUGAR FIX

A very refreshing cake that is even better with fresh whipped cream or cream cheese frosting.

Orange Cake

350°   35 minutes

3 cups cake flour
1 ½ cups sugar
1 Tbsp. baking powder
½ tsp. baking soda
½ tsp. salt
2 Tbsp. orange gelatin
1 cup butter, softened
1 ¼ cup buttermilk
2 eggs
2 tsp. real vanilla
1 tsp. orange flavoring

Sift together flour, sugar, baking powder, baking soda, salt, and orange gelatin powder. Add butter and 1 cup of the buttermilk. Mix slowly until combined then beat at medium speed for 90 seconds. Meanwhile, mix eggs, vanilla, and orange flavoring with remaining buttermilk. Scrape down sides. Add to batter; mixing in two batches for about 20 seconds each. Pour into 2 - 8" or one 9"x13" prepared pan(s). Bake at 350° for 35 minutes. Allow cakes to cool for 10 minutes before turning out onto cooling racks. Allow cakes to cool completely before frosting.

Try pouring freshly made, slightly cooled orange gelatin over hot cake, then frosting with Sweetened Whipped Cream or whipped topping.

Cakes

I don't know of anyone who does not like this cake. It's a great cake for last minute desserts and for chocolate lovers. This cake is fabulous if eaten while still warm. My youngest son and father-in-law ask for this cake for almost every birthday.

Chocolate Sheet Cake

350°   *20 mins.*

½ cup butter
½ cup peanut oil*
1 cup water
5 Tbsp. cocoa
½ cup buttermilk
2 eggs
2 tsp. vanilla
3 cups cake flour
2 cups sugar
1 tsp. baking soda
½ tsp. salt
1 tsp. cinnamon

In small saucepan, bring to boil first four ingredients. Meanwhile, stir together dry ingredients; set aside. Combine buttermilk, eggs, and vanilla. When chocolate mixture boils add it to the flour; then add the buttermilk mixture. Pour into prepared sheet pan and bake for 20 minutes. Five minutes before cake is to come out of the oven begin making the frosting (page 38).

<u>*For those with peanut allergies, substitute cooking oil or butter.</u>

THE SUGAR FIX

This delicious cake has a beautiful pink color, which makes it perfect for birthday cakes for little girls or baby girl shower cakes.

Strawberry Cake

350°　　　　　　　　　　　　　　　　*35 minutes*

3 cups cake flour
1 ½ cups sugar
1 Tbsp. baking powder
½ tsp. baking soda
½ tsp. salt
2 Tbsp. strawberry gelatin
1 cup butter, softened
1 ¼ cup buttermilk
2 eggs
2 tsp. real vanilla

Sift together flour, sugar, baking powder, baking soda, salt, and strawberry gelatin powder. Add butter and 1 cup of the buttermilk. Mix slowly until combined then beat at medium speed for 90 seconds. Meanwhile, mix eggs and vanilla with remaining buttermilk. Scrape down sides. Add to batter; mixing in two batches for about 20 seconds each. Pour into 2 - 8" or one 9"x13" prepared pan(s). Bake at 350° for 35 minutes. Allow cakes to cool for 10 minutes before turning out onto cooling racks. Allow cakes to cool completely before frosting. Frost with White Buttercream Frosting or White Chocolate Frosting (page 34).

Cakes

Dynasty

Another cake for the Oklahoma State Sugar Art Show, this one was a Wedding Fit for a Queen. The cake is gold with red peonies, orange blossoms, and dark green bamboo leaves. Each peony has 25 individually made petals and the whole piece took 6 months to make! Being obsessive-compulsive, I even made the cake stand, and the background. The symbols on the fan (to the left) mean true love and the symbol on the cake means eternity.

THE SUGAR FIX

I have never like pineapple upside-down cake. Then while trying to come up with on for a cake order, I tried it and I loved it. My customer was also quite happy with it as well. Always use pineapple slices packed in their juices rather than in syrup.

Pineapple Upside-Down Cake

325⁰   30 minutes

½ cup butter
1 cup dark brown sugar
20 oz. can pineapple slices, drained (reserve juice)
½ cup toasted, chopped pecans
10 maraschino cherries, halved
1 ½ cups cake flour
1 ½ tsp. baking powder
½ tsp. salt
1 cup sugar
4 eggs, separated
¼ cup buttermilk
2 Tbsp. butter, melted
1 tsp. almond extract
2 tsp. vanilla

Melt ½ cup butter in 10" square pan. Evenly sprinkle brown sugar over melted butter. Arrange pineapple slices neatly over sugar. Place ½ of a cherry; cut side up inside pineapple rings. Sprinkle pecans evenly in the pan. Set aside. Beat egg whites until foamy, then slowly add sugar; beating to stiff peaks. Sift together flour, baking powder, and salt. Beat egg yolks until thick and lemon colored. Add flour mixture alternately with pineapple juice. Add buttermilk, 2 Tbsp. melted butter, almond extract, and vanilla. Fold in 1/3 of the whites; mix well. Add remaining egg whites, folding gently until there are no streaks. Pour over pineapple slices and bake for 30-35 minutes. Cool 5 minutes before inverting onto platter.

Try this cake next time you want something moist and flavorful for a church or work social. You just might be the hit of the party.

Buttermilk Pound Cake

325°   1 hour 15 minutes

1 ½ cup butter, softened
2 ½ cups sugar
4 eggs
1 Tbsp. rum
2 tsp. vanilla
1 tsp. almond extract
3 ½ cups cake flour
½ tsp. baking soda
½ tsp. salt
1 cup buttermilk

Cream butter and sugar, beating until fluffy. Add eggs, one at a time, beating well after each. Add rum, vanilla, and almond extract. Sift together flour, baking soda, and salt. Add alternately with buttermilk, beginning and ending with flour. Pour into prepared Bundt pan and bake for 1 hour 20 minutes. Cool 15 minutes, then turn out onto wire rack to cool completely. Place on serving plate, then drizzle with Vanilla or Rum Glaze, page 51.

Autumn Splendor

When I take a class with Eleanor Rielander of South Africa, we always make completed display. I always love her class. The white flowers are called iceberg roses and the small flowers are orange tipped Crocosmia Aurea. I added the butterfly and the acorns to give it an autumn look. I received 3rd Place at the 2003 Oklahoma State Sugar Art Show. Not bad for a class project.

I have a friend that will go off her diet for this cake. She has requested that I not make it very often. It's a great cake, but a little more complicated than the others. This is definitely a special occasion cake.

Chocolate Chip Cake

325°   30 minutes

8 eggs, separated
1 ½ cups sugar, divided
1 cup butter, creamy soft
2 tsp. vanilla
1 ½ cups sifted cake flour
2 tsp. baking powder
1 tsp. baking soda
½ tsp. salt
¾ cup buttermilk
10 oz. grated semi-sweet chocolate

Beat egg whites with ½ cup sugar to stiff, but not dry peaks. Set aside. Beat egg yolks with 1 cup sugar at high speed until smooth and lemon colored. Add butter and vanilla; mix well. Sift together cake flour, baking powder, baking soda, and salt. Add alternately with buttermilk, beginning and ending with flour mixture. Stir in chocolate. Fold in 1/3 of the whites until smooth. Fold in remaining whites, stirring until there are no streaks. Pour into 3-8" round pans that are lined with parchment or waxed paper and pan coating. Bake for 25-30 minutes, or until toothpick comes out clean. Cool for 10 minutes on wire rack. Remove from pans and allow to cool completely before frosting. Frost with Old Fashioned Frosting (page 39).

THE SUGAR FIX

My oldest son, Jason, always asks for this cake for his birthday. It's a great cake warm or room temperature. Jason likes to warm it up in the microwave for about 30 seconds to melt the glaze. What a great idea!

Lemon Pound Cake

325°   1 hr. 15 minutes

3 cups cake flour
½ tsp. salt
¼ tsp. baking powder
1 cup butter
3 cups sugar
6 eggs
2 tsp. lemon extract
2 tsp. vanilla
1 cup buttermilk

Sift together flour, salt, and baking powder; set aside. Cream butter and sugar until light and fluffy. Add eggs, one at a time, beating a total of 10 minutes on low speed. Add lemon extract and vanilla; mix well. Add dry ingredients alternately with buttermilk, beginning and ending with flour. Pour into prepared Bundt pan. Bake for 1 hour 15 minutes. Cool 15 minutes, then turn out onto wire rack. Cool completely. Place onto serving plate and drizzle with Lemon Glaze, page 51.

Cakes

An old fashioned version of a spice cake. This one is moist and delicious, especially when frosted with Cream Cheese Frosting or Spiced Cream Cheese Frosting.

Applesauce Cake

350° *35 minutes*

3 cups cake flour
1 ½ tsp. baking soda
¼ tsp. baking powder
½ tsp. salt
1 tsp. ground cinnamon
½ tsp. ground cloves
½ tsp. ground allspice
¼ tsp. ground ginger
½ cup butter, softened
2 cups brown sugar
2 eggs
2 cups applesauce
½ cup chopped, toasted pecans

Sift together flour, baking soda, baking powder, salt, cinnamon, cloves, allspice, and ginger. Cream butter and sugar until light and fluffy. Add eggs, one at a time, mixing well after each. Add flour alternately with applesauce, beginning and ending with flour, mixing well after each addition. Stir in pecans, then pour into 2-9"x2" round prepared pans. Bake for 35 minutes or until toothpick comes out clean. Cool on wire rack for 10 minutes. Turn out onto wire rack to cool completely.

Frostings

White Buttercream Frosting 32
White Chocolate Buttercream Frosting 32
Lemon Buttercream Frosting 34
Chocolate Buttercream Frosting 34
Chocolate Amaretto Buttercream Frosting 35
Double Fudge Buttercream Frosting 35
Ginger Hint Fudge Frosting 36
Chocolate Sheet Cake Frosting 36
Old Fashioned Frosting 37
Cream Cheese Frosting 37
Spiced Cream Cheese Frosting 38
Coconut Cake Cream Frosting 38
Vanilla Fondant 39
White Chocolate Fondant 40
Chocolate Fondant 42
Ginger Chocolate Fondant 44
Lemon Fondant 45
Italian Buttercream 47
Chocolate Italian Buttercream 48
Sweetened Whipped Cream 48
Vanilla Glaze 49
Lemon Glaze 49
Rum Glaze 49
Chocolate Glaze 50
Chocolate Amaretto Glaze 50
Royal Icing 51

White Buttercream Frosting

1 cup butter, softened
1 cup shortening
½ tsp. salt
½ cup heavy cream
2 tsp. clear vanilla*
4 cups sifted powdered sugar

Cream butter, shortening, and white chocolate. Add salt, cream, and real vanilla; mix until combined. Add powdered sugar; mix slowly until combined; then beat on medium speed (high if using hand mixer) for one minute.

*Use real vanilla for an ivory color.

White Chocolate Buttercream Frosting

4 oz. white chocolate, melted and cooled
1 cup butter, softened
1 cup shortening
½ tsp. salt
½ cup heavy cream
2 tsp. clear vanilla
2 lbs. powdered sugar

In large mixer bowl, combine white chocolate, butter, shortening, salt, cream, and vanilla. Add powdered sugar. Mix slowly until just combined, then at high speed for 1 minute.

Frostings

Frog Wedding Cake

I made this cake just for fun to enter in the April 2000 Texas Sugar Art Show. I thought the judges would not like it because it was silly. Little did I know that they would love it I received 1ˢᵗ Place, Best of Division, and Best of Show.

All of the decorations are edible, including the "sand". It was made with ground cookies, crackers, and brown sugar.

Lemon Buttercream Frosting

1 cup butter, softened
1 cup shortening
½ tsp. salt
¼ lemon juice
¼ cup heavy cream
1 tsp. lemon extract
2 tsp. clear vanilla
2 lbs. powdered sugar

In large mixer bowl, cream butter, shortening, and salt. Add lemon juice, cream, lemon extract, and vanilla; mix well. Add powdered sugar; mix slowly until just combined, then on high speed for 1 minute.

Chocolate Buttercream Frosting

1 cup butter, softened
1 cup shortening
½ tsp. salt
2/3 cup heavy cream
2 tsp. vanilla
2 lbs. powdered sugar
½ cup cocoa

In large mixer bowl, combine butter, shortening, salt, cream, and vanilla. Add powdered sugar and cocoa. Mix slowly until just combined, then at high speed for 1 minute.

Frostings

Chocolate Amaretto Buttercream Frosting

>1 cup butter, softened
>1 cup shortening
>½ tsp. salt
>½ cup heavy cream
>3 Tbsp. amaretto
>2 tsp. vanilla
>2 lbs. powdered sugar
>½ cup cocoa

In large mixer bowl, combine butter, shortening, salt, cream, amaretto, and vanilla. Add powdered sugar and cocoa. Mix slowly until just combined, then at high speed for 1 minute.

Double Fudge Buttercream Frosting

>½ cup semi-sweet chocolate chips, melted and cooled
>1 cup butter, softened
>1 cup shortening
>½ tsp. salt
>2/3 cup heavy cream
>2 tsp. vanilla
>2 lbs. powdered sugar
>½ cup cocoa

In large mixer bowl, combine melted chocolate, butter, shortening, salt, cream, and vanilla. Add powdered sugar and cocoa. Mix slowly until just combined, then at high speed for 1 minute.

When I am entering a tasting division, there is no telling what I will decide to make. This is one of those attempts. I believe I won second place for the entire entry of Ginger Chocolate Cake (page 48), this frosting, and Ginger Chocolate Fondant (page 48). The theme that year was a groom's cake.

THE SUGAR FIX

Ginger Hint Fudge Frosting

1 cup butter, softened
1 cup shortening
½ cup cream
2 tsp. vanilla powder
½ tsp. ginger
½ tsp. salt
1 cup Jersey cocoa
2 lbs. powdered sugar

Cream butter and shortening. Add cream, vanilla powder, ginger, and salt. Mix well. Add cocoa and powdered sugar. Mix slowly until combined, then beat at high speed for 1 minute.

Chocolate Sheet Cake Frosting

½ cup butter
5 Tbsp. cocoa
½ cup heavy cream*
¼ tsp. salt
4-5 cups powdered sugar
2 tsp. vanilla
½ cup chopped pecans

Bring to boil butter, cocoa, cream, and salt. Add 4 cups sifted powdered sugar (adjust as needed). Frosting should be thick but still pourable. Stir in pecans and vanilla. Spread over hot cake.

* Milk or ½ & ½ can be used in place of the cream.

Frostings

Old Fashioned Frosting

1 ½ cups butter, softened
2/3 cup half & half
3 tsp. vanilla
1 cup dutched cocoa
½ tsp. salt
2 lb. powdered sugar

In large mixer bowl, combine butter, half & half, and vanilla. Add cocoa, salt, and powdered sugar. Mix on low until dry ingredients are incorporated, then beat on high until light and fluffy.

Cream Cheese Frosting

1 cup butter, softened
8 oz. pkg. cream cheese, softened
1 tsp. real vanilla*
½ tsp. salt
2 lbs. sifted powdered sugar

Cream butter and cream cheese. Add salt and vanilla. Mix well. Add powdered sugar; mix slowly until combined then beat on high for one minute.

*Use clear vanilla for a whiter frosting

Spiced Cream Cheese Frosting

1 cup butter, softened
8 oz. pkg. cream cheese, softened
1 tsp. ground cinnamon
¼ tsp. ground allspice
¼ tsp. ground ginger
¼ tsp. ground cloves
1 tsp. real vanilla
½ tsp. salt
2 lbs. sifted powdered sugar

Cream butter and cream cheese. Add spices and salt. Mix well. Add powdered sugar; mix slowly until combined then beat on high for one minute.

Coconut Cake Cream Frosting

1 cup butter, softened
2 – 8 oz. pkg. cream cheese, softened
2 lbs. powdered sugar, sifted
2 tsp. vanilla, clear for whiter frosting
¼ tsp. salt
½ cup chopped, toasted pecans
1 ½ cups toasted coconut

Cream butter and cream cheese. Gradually add powdered sugar; then add vanilla and salt. Beat on high for 1 minute or until fluffy. Spread between layers and on cake. Garnish with pecans and toasted coconut.

Frostings

Fondant has been given a negative view based on a few poorly made commercial products. This fondant is delicious, versatile, and easy to use. It does take some time to make, but is well worth the effort. It is also less expensive than commercial.

Vanilla Fondant

½ cup cream
3 pkg. unflavored gelatin
1 cup corn syrup
3 Tbsp. butter
3 Tbsp. glycerin
2 tsp. clear vanilla
dash salt
3-4 lbs. powdered sugar

Combine cream and gelatin. Allow to firm. Cook over double boiler until gelatin is dissolved. Add remaining ingredients and cook until butter is almost melted. Allow to cool to luke warm. Strain into large mixer bowl containing 2 lbs. powdered sugar. Mix by hand until just combined. Add several more cups of powdered sugar. Using dough hook, mix on low until combined. Continue adding powdered sugar until fondant holds its shape on hook. Turn out onto powdered sugar-covered surface, kneading until smooth. Wrap in plastic wrap "painted" with cooking oil. Wrap again in plastic wrap (no oil), then store in a plastic zipper bag. Let stand 24 hours before using.

> If the gelatin mixture cools too much or you find you don't have time to finish, place plastic wrap over the container, refrigerate, then warm in the microwave when you are ready to use it.

THE SUGAR FIX

This fondant and the next are unbelievably delicious. The white chocolate in particular tastes wonderful over vanilla or lemon buttercream, and cream cheese frostings.

White Chocolate Fondant

½ cup cream
3 pkg. unflavored gelatin
1 cup corn syrup
3 Tbsp. butter
3 Tbsp. glycerin
2 tsp. vanilla
dash salt
½ cup white chocolate pieces
3-4 lbs. powdered sugar

Combine milk and gelatin. Allow to firm. Cook over double boiler until gelatin is dissolved. Add remaining ingredients and cook until butter is almost melted. Allow to cool to luke warm. Strain into large mixer bowl containing 2 lbs. powdered sugar. Mix by hand until just combined. Add several more cups of powdered sugar. Using dough hook, mix on low until combined. Continue adding powdered sugar until fondant holds its shape on hook. Turn out onto powdered sugar-covered surface, kneading until smooth. Wrap in plastic wrap "painted" with cooking oil. Wrap again in plastic wrap (no oil), then store in plastic zipper bag. Let stand 24 hours before using.

Any of the fondants can be made with half & half, milk, or even water. The butter can be replace with shortening for a whiter fondant.
The white chocolate fondant will be a very light cream color.

Frostings

The Chocolate Shoppe

I received 1ˢᵗ Place at the 2003 Oklahoma State Sugar Art Show for this chocolate gingerbread house. The roof tiles are made with white chocolate and dark chocolate fondant, each one very carefully cut. I used royal icing to make the window details. As you can see, the obsessive-compulsive tendencies spill out onto gingerbread house making as well.

THE SUGAR FIX

This fondant is perfect for groom's cakes or for making chocolate gumpaste (page 125) for wonderfully different decorations on your cakes.

Chocolate Fondant

½ cup milk
3 pkg. unflavored gelatin
1 cup corn syrup
3 Tbsp. butter
3 Tbsp. glycerin
2 tsp. vanilla
dash salt
½ cup dark chocolate pieces
3-4 lbs. powdered sugar

Combine milk and gelatin. Allow to firm. Cook over double boiler until gelatin is dissolved. Add remaining ingredients and cook until butter is almost melted. Allow to cool to luke warm. Strain into large mixer bowl containing 2 lbs. powdered sugar. Mix by hand until just combined. Add several more cups of powdered sugar. Using dough hook, mix on low until combined. Continue adding powdered sugar until fondant holds its shape on hook. Turn out onto powdered sugar-covered surface, kneading until smooth. Wrap in plastic wrap "painted" with cooking oil. Wrap again in plastic wrap (no oil), then store in plastic zipper bag. Let stand 24 hours before using.

Frostings

The Perfect Apology

What better way to tell someone you're sorry than to give her a bouquet of chocolate flowers? Surely a lady couldn't stay angry after receiving this.
I won 1ˢᵗ Place and People's Choice at the 2002 Chocolate Festival in Norman, Oklahoma. It's still as beautiful now as it was then.

THE SUGAR FIX

This is another one of those experiment recipes for the ginger, chocolate, and vanilla competition at the Oklahoma Sugar Art Show.

Ginger Chocolate Fondant

½ cup milk
3 pkg. unflavored gelatin
1 cup corn syrup
3 Tbsp. butter
3 Tbsp. glycerin
2 tsp. vanilla bean paste
dash salt
½ cup dark chocolate pieces
2 Tbsp. ginger
3-4 lbs. powdered sugar

Combine milk and gelatin. Allow to firm. Cook over double boiler until gelatin is dissolved. Add remaining ingredients and cook until butter is almost melted. Allow to cool to luke warm. Strain into large mixer bowl containing 2 lbs. powdered sugar. Mix by hand until just combined. Add several more cups of powdered sugar. Using dough hook, mix on low until combined. Continue adding powdered sugar until fondant holds its shape on hook. Turn out onto powdered sugar-covered surface, kneading until smooth. Wrap in plastic wrap "painted" with cooking oil. Wrap again in plastic wrap (no oil), then store in plastic zipper bag. Let stand 24 hours before using.

Frostings

This is one of my favorite flavors for fondant. It tastes great on lemon, white, or orange cakes. It is not yellow, but can easily be made yellow with <u>paste</u> food coloring during the cooking or mixing process.

Lemon Fondant

½ cup cream
3 pkg. unflavored gelatin
1 cup corn syrup
3 Tbsp. butter
3 Tbsp. glycerin
2 tsp. clear vanilla*
dash salt
¼ cup lemon juice
1 tsp. lemon extract
3-4 lbs. powdered sugar

Combine cream and gelatin. Allow to firm. Cook over double boiler until gelatin is dissolved. Add remaining ingredients and cook until butter is almost melted. Allow to cool to luke warm. Strain into large mixer bowl containing 2 lbs. powdered sugar. Mix by hand until just combined. Add several more cups of powdered sugar. Using dough hook, mix on low until combined. Continue adding powdered sugar until fondant holds its shape on hook. Turn out onto powdered sugar-covered surface, kneading until smooth. Wrap in plastic wrap "painted" with cooking oil. Wrap again in plastic wrap (no oil), then store in zipper bag. Let stand 24 hours before using.

*Use real vanilla for an ivory color.

THE SUGAR FIX

Elegant Wedding Cake

I was on cloud nine on my way home from the Texas Sugar Art Show when I won my first Best of Show with this cake. I had also won first place on everything I had entered! It could not have been a better weekend!

Frostings

For those who do not like the sweetness of regular buttercream, this is the frosting for them. It is more expensive and time consuming to make, but it is unbelievably delicious. The cake will need to be refrigerated for storage, but tastes best at room temperature.

Italian Buttercream

1 ½ cups sugar
1/3 cup water
dash salt
4 egg whites
1 ½ to 2 cups butter, softened
2 tsp. vanilla

Combine sugar and water in small heavy saucepan; cook over medium heat without stirring until temperature reaches 234º. While sugar is cooking beat egg whites to soft peaks. Remove pan from heat. With mixer off, pour small amount of hot sugar into egg whites; then beat at high speed for 10 seconds. Continue doing this with remaining sugar. Beat at high speed for 10 minutes. Add butter in small amounts; mixing on low speed. When mixture begins to thicken, beat on high until fluffy. Mixture will look very thin, but will suddenly fluff up. Add vanilla. Mix on high until fluffy.

THE SUGAR FIX

Chocolate Italian Buttercream

1 ½ cups sugar
1/3 cup water
dash salt
4 egg whites
1 ½ to 2 cups butter, softened
2 tsp. vanilla
½ tsp. almond extract
3 oz. semi-sweet chocolate, melted and cooled

Combine sugar and water in small heavy saucepan; cook over medium heat without stirring until temperature reaches 234º. While sugar is cooking beat egg whites to soft peaks. Remove pan from heat. With mixer off, pour small amount of hot sugar into egg whites; then beat at high speed for 10 seconds. Continue doing this with remaining sugar. Beat at high speed for 10 minutes. Add butter in small amounts; mixing on low speed. When mixture begins to thicken beat on high until fluffy. Mixture will look very thin, but will suddenly fluff up. Add vanilla, almond extract, and chocolate. Mix on high until fluffy.

Sweetened Whipped Cream

2 cups heavy cream, very cold
¼ cup sifted powdered sugar
1 tsp. vanilla extract

Chill large mixing bowl and whip until very cold. Place all three ingredients in bowl. Whip on high speed until just fluffy. Serve on cakes, pies, fruit, or hot chocolate. Place any left over in airtight bowl and use within two days.

Vanilla Glaze

2 cups powdered sugar, sifted
1 Tbsp. milk
½ tsp. vanilla

Slowly add milk to powdered sugar to make a heavy, but pourable glaze, then add vanilla. Adjust amount of milk as needed. Drizzle over cake, allowing it to run down the sides and center.

Lemon Glaze

2 cups powdered sugar, sifted
1 Tbsp. lemon juice
½ tsp. vanilla
1 tsp. lemon extract

Slowly add lemon juice to powdered sugar to make a heavy, but pourable glaze, then add vanilla and lemon extract. Adjust amount of lemon juice as needed. Drizzle over cake, allowing it to run down the sides and center.

Rum Glaze

2 cups powdered sugar, sifted
1 Tbsp. milk
½ tsp. vanilla
1 Tbsp. rum

Slowly add milk to powdered sugar to make a heavy, but pourable glaze, then add vanilla and rum. Adjust amount of milk as needed. Drizzle over cake, allowing it to run down the sides and center.

Chocolate Glaze

½ cup butter
½ cup evaporated milk
2 tsp. vanilla
½ tsp. salt
4 cups powdered sugar, sifted
½ cup cocoa, sifted

Beat butter, evaporated milk, vanilla, and salt until smooth. Add powdered sugar and cocoa slowly; mix until smooth. Pour over cooled cake.

Chocolate Amaretto Glaze

½ cup butter
½ cup evaporated milk
2 Tbsp. Amaretto
½ tsp. almond extract
2 tsp. vanilla
½ tsp. salt
4 cups powdered sugar, sifted
½ cup cocoa, sifted

Beat butter, evaporated milk, amaretto, almond extract, vanilla, and salt until smooth. Add powdered sugar and cocoa slowly; mix until smooth. Pour over cooled cake.

Frostings

Royal Icing

4 cups powdered sugar, sifted
3 Tbsp. powdered egg whites
1-2 Tbsp. water*

In large mixer bowl, slowly mix powdered sugar and powdered egg whites using whisk attachment. All water slowly while mixer is running until combined. Beat on high for 3 minutes or until fluffy.

*Water will need to be adjusted according to current humidity and desired consistency. Add more water in very small amounts to make "run-out" frosting for use decorating cookies.

If you are brave enough or crazy enough to try string-work or embroidery work on your fondant cakes, thin with clear corn syrup. Since the tips for these techniques are tiny, strain icing through the foot of a new knee-high hose into the frosting bag that is already fitted with the tip. This removes any lumps that will invariably clog your tips to the point of madness.

☺

Pies

Apple Pie Filling	54
Pecan Pie	55
Cherry Pie Filling	56
Vanilla Cream Pie	57
Lemon Pie	58
Chocolate Cream Pie	59
Italian Meringue	60
Quick & Easy Lemon Pie	61
Key Lime Pie	62
Caramel Pie Filling	63
Basic Pie Crust	64
Cookie Crust	65
Graham Cracker Crust	65
Chocolate Cookie Crust	66
Coconut/Cookie Crust	66

THE SUGAR FIX

For me, most apple pies are too bland, but this one is <u>spicy</u>. I love it also because the apples are sliced very thinly, so I know they will be done. If you like a less spicy pie, just reduce the amounts of spices by half. Don't forget to put the cinnamon/sugar on the top for a sweet crunch.

Apple Pie Filling

6-8 Rome apples, peeled, cored and thinly sliced
1 cup sugar
2 Tbsp. flour
½ tsp. ground cloves
½ tsp. ground allspice
1 tsp. ground cinnamon
¼ tsp. ground ginger
2 Tbsp. butter
2 Tbsp. butter, melted
cinnamon /sugar mix

Combine dry ingredients; add apples. Pour into unbaked 9" pastry; dot with butter, then cover with top crust. Seal edges and cut vent holes in crust. Brush with melted butter and sprinkle with cinnamon and sugar. Bake in 350F oven for 1 hour 15 minutes. Place pie plate on a cookie sheet to catch any spill over. Pie crust recipe is on page 66.

Miniature cookie cutters are great for making the vent hole and for add crust decorations to your double crust pies.

Pies

My mom always made great pies, so it's no surprise that this one goes fast during the holidays. For easier slicing, pecan can be coarsely chopped.

Pecan Pie

350º   40 minutes

3 eggs
2/3 cup sugar
½ tsp. Salt
1/3 cup melted butter
¾ cup corn syrup
2 tsp. Vanilla
¾ cup pecan halves

In medium mixing bowl, combine eggs, sugar, salt, butter, corn syrup, and vanilla. Add pecans. Pour into unbaked pie shell. Bake for 40 to 50 minutes until set and brown. Let cool, then store in refrigerator.

One-inch strips of aluminum foil on the edges of the crust will prevent over-baking.

THE SUGAR FIX

Almond flavoring brings out the true flavor of the cherries in this pie recipe. If you like, brush a little melted butter and sprinkle a little bit of granulated sugar on the crust before baking.

Cherry Pie Filling

350° Makes 2-9" pies

1 cup sugar
¼ cup flour
¼ tsp. salt
¾ cup cherry juice (from can)
3 ½ cup cherries (drained)
2 Tbsp. butter
½ tsp. almond extract
1 tsp. vanilla

Mix together sugar, flour, and salt. Add cherry juice and cook over medium heat until thickens and boils. Pour sauce over cherries; mix well. Pour into unbaked 9" pie shell, dot with butter. Place top crust over pie, seal edges, and cut vent holes to allow steam to escape. Bake for 40 minutes. To prevent boil over mess, bake pie on a cookie sheet.

Make a double batch of the pie crust on page 46 and divide in half for this pie.

Pies

Try this for a very rich, smooth pie or pudding. It can be used with chocolate or coconut pie fillings to make a wonderful parfait.

Vanilla Cream Pie

1 cup sugar
½ cup flour
½ tsp. salt
3 cups milk
4 eggs
3 Tbsp. butter
2 tsp. vanilla

In medium saucepan, stir together sugar, flour, and salt. Stir in milk. Cook on medium high heat until thickened and bubbly. Reduce heat to medium and cook 2 minutes more. Remove from heat. Separate eggs, slightly beat yolks and set aside whites. Add about 1 cup of chocolate mixture to yolks; mix well. Add back to chocolate, cook to gentle boil, then 2 minutes more. Remove from heat; add butter and vanilla. Stir until butter is melted. Pour into bowl through strainer. Cover with plastic wrap touching pudding. Chill overnight. Pour into 9" baked pie shell and cover with whipped cream or meringue. Serve cold.

Try adding a couple of tablespoons of rum or amaretto for a very unique flavor that will have everyone trying to guess your secret.

THE SUGAR FIX

Fresh whipped cream is a mellow alternative to meringue. If you prefer meringue, save the egg whites and follow the recipe on page (). Chilling the filling before putting in the piecrust will prevent the crust becoming soggy. A blowtorch works great for browning meringue without heating up the pie.

Lemon Pie

1 ½ cups sugar
¼ cup corn starch
¼ cup flour
½ tsp. salt
1 ½ cups water
3 jumbo eggs, separated
3 Tbsp. butter
1/3 cup fresh lemon juice
1 tsp. lemon extract
2 tsp. vanilla

In medium saucepan combine sugar, starch, flour, and salt. Gradually stir in water. Cook and stir over medium-high heat until thickened and bubbly. Reduce heat; cook and stir for 2 minutes more. Remove from heat. Beat yolks slightly, then stir about 1 cup of hot mixture into the yolks. Return to hot mixture. Cook and stir over medium heat; bring to gentle boil. Cook 2 minutes more. Remove from heat. Add lemon juice, butter, lemon extract, and vanilla. Place in bowl through strainer; cover with plastic wrap touching filling. Chill overnight. When cold, pour into baked pie shell; then top with fresh whipped cream. Serve cold.

To make this a prettier pie when cut, add a little bit of yellow food coloring during the cooking process.

Pies

One of my customers requested whipped cream on their chocolate pie order instead of meringue and I was hooked. It tastes wonderful and no meringue to weep.

Chocolate Cream Pie

1 ½ cups sugar
½ cup flour
½ tsp. salt
3 cups milk
1 cup chocolate chips
4 eggs
¼ cup butter
3 tsp. vanilla

In medium saucepan, stir together sugar, flour, and salt. Stir in milk and chocolate chips. Cook on medium high heat until thickened and bubbly. Reduce heat to medium and cook 2 minutes more. Remove from heat. Separate eggs, slightly beat yolks and set aside whites. Add about 1 cup of chocolate mixture to yolks; mix well. Add back to chocolate, cook to gentle boil, then 2 minutes more. Remove from heat; add butter and vanilla. Stir until butter is melted. Pour into bowl through strainer. Cover with plastic wrap touching pudding. Chill overnight. Pour into 9" baked pie shell and cover with whipped cream or meringue. Serve cold.

---

8 oz. of semi-sweet chocolate squares can be used in place of the chocolate chips, but they must be chopped into smaller pieces.

THE SUGAR FIX

This meringue takes longer to make, but it is less like to "weep" or make those sticky droplets that we all hate. It also tastes a lot like divinity! It can be put on a hot or cold pie filling.

Italian Meringue

1 ½ cups sugar
1/3 cup water
dash salt
4 egg whites
2 tsp. vanilla

Combine sugar and water in a small heavy saucepan; cook over medium heat without stirring until temperature reaches 234º. While sugar is cooking, beat egg whites to soft peaks. Remove pan from heat. With mixer turned off, pour a small amount of hot sugar into egg whites; then beat at high speed for 10 seconds. Continue doing this with remaining sugar. Beat at high speed for 10 minutes. Spread over pie, then brown in 375º for 5 minutes or until desired brownness.

A small blow torch works wonderfully to brown the meringue quickly without heating the entire pie.

This pie is very creamy and delicious. It is also very easy to make. Try it when you need a dessert at the last minute for home or socials.

Quick & Easy Lemon Pie

1 - 9" graham cracker crust or cookie crust
1 14-oz. can sweetened condensed milk
1/3 cup fresh lemon juice
½ tsp. lemon extract
1 tsp. vanilla
1-2 drops yellow food coloring
2 cups fresh whipped cream or whipped topping

Mix together sweetened condensed milk, lemon juice, lemon extract, vanilla, and food coloring. Fold in whipped cream or whipped topping. Pour into pie shell. Chill for 2 hours, then add more whipped cream for decoration.

If you are really in a hurry, try using the pre-made graham cracker crusts available at the supermarket.

THE SUGAR FIX

For a quick and easy pie, this one can't be beat. It's also great for tarts. Pipe a decorative edge of whipped cream to make it appear as if you spent a lot of time and effort on them.

Key Lime Pie

2 - 9" graham cracker crust or cookie crust
1 14-oz. can sweetened condensed milk
¼ cup fresh lime juice
1 tsp. vanilla
1-2 drops green food coloring
2 cups fresh whipped cream or whipped topping

Mix together sweetened condensed milk, lime juice, vanilla, and food coloring. Fold in whipped cream. Pour into pie shell. Chill for 2 hours, then add more whipped cream for decoration.

The Coconut Cookie Crust on page 48 would be an unusual alternative that your family will love.

Pies

Not only is this a great pie, but it makes a great filling for cakes. Check out the recipe for Chocolate Earthquake on page 64.

Caramel Pie Filling

¼ cup butter
¼ cup all-purpose flour
½ cup dark brown sugar
½ cup sugar
½ tsp. salt
1 egg
1 cup heavy cream
2 tsp. vanilla

In large, heavy saucepan, cream butter, flour, brown sugar, sugar, and salt. Mix together egg and cream; add to butter mixture. Cook over medium heat, stirring constantly until thickened and barely bubbly. Remove from heat. Cool, add vanilla, and beat with electric mixer until smooth. Pour into prepared 9" pie shell. Top with whipped cream.

THE SUGAR FIX

I have to admit that my mom came up with this recipe. She is a self-taught cook and an excellent one at that. We grew up with great dinners and great desserts. Mom always made our favorite things for our birthdays. Thanks, Mom.

Basic Pie Crust

425⁰ *15 minutes*

1 cup all-purpose flour
½ tsp. salt
½ cup shortening
¼ cup cold water

Stir together flour and salt. Cut in shortening until mixture is crumbly. Add cold water and stir until just combined. Form into a ball, place on floured surface and roll to about a 12" circle. DO NOT ROLL MORE THAN ONE TIME. Re-rolling will cause the crust to be tough. Gently lift and lay the crust into pie plate. Slightly trim edges leaving enough to roll under for a neat finish. After rolling crust under press to edge of the pie plate with your thumb. Using the back of a sharp knife, trim rough edges of crust. If making a pre-baked pie crust, poke holes randomly to allow steam to escape. Bake for 15 minutes. Allow to cool. This crust can be frozen before and after baking.

Use a heavy muslin piece about 24" x 24" to roll out pie crust. Dust liberally with flour.

Pies

Cookie Crust

375⁰   *10 minutes*

Approximately 25 vanilla wafers
1 Tbsp. sugar
¼ cup butter, melted
½ tsp. vanilla

Crush cookies in a food processor to fine crumbs. Add sugar, butter, and vanilla. Process until just combined. Press into 9" pie plate. Bake for 10 minutes. Allow to cool before filing.

Graham Cracker Crust

375⁰   *10 minutes*

1celephane wrapped package graham crackers
2 Tbsp. sugar
¼ cup butter, melted
½ tsp. vanilla

Crush crackers in a food processor to fine crumbs. Add sugar, butter, and vanilla. Process until just combined. Press into 9" pie plate. Bake for 10 minutes. Allow to cool before filing.

If you do not have a food processor, crush the cookies or crackers in a plastic zipper bag.
Use a rolling pin to make the crumbs fine.

THE SUGAR FIX

When I had the shop, I used this recipe with the Pecan Caramel Cheesecake (page 78). It is now my stepdaughter's request for her birthday.

Chocolate Cookie Crust

375⁰   10 minutes

Approximately 25 chocolate sandwich cookies
1 Tbsp. sugar
¼ cup butter, melted
½ tsp. vanilla

Crush cookies in a food processor to fine crumbs. Add sugar, butter, and vanilla. Process until just combined. Press into 9" pie plate. Bake for 10 minutes. Allow to cool before filing.

Use this crust for the Piña Colada Cheesecake (page 56) or even a plain cheesecake (page 62). It's great!

Coconut/Cookie Crust

350⁰

35 vanilla wafers, crushed
2 Tbsp. sugar
¼ cup melted butter
1 tsp. vanilla
½ cup toasted coconut

Crush cookies in food processor; add sugar, butter, and vanilla. Process until just combined. Stir in coconut by hand. Press into bottom of prepared spring form pan. For easier removal onto serving plate, also line the bottom with parchment paper or waxed paper.

If you are going to use any of these crusts for cheesecake, do not bake it before filling. It will make the crust very hard.

Desserts

Baked Fudge	68
Piňa Colada Cheesecake	69
Topping	70
Lemon Bars	71
Marshmallow Whirl Brownies	72
Ginger Crunch Bars	73
Pecan Crunch Bars	74
Caramel Sauce	75
Cheesecake	76
Caramel Pecan Cheesecake	77
Chocolate Earthquake	78
Apple Crisp	79
Creamy Chocolate Torte	80
Chocolate Sauce	80
Orange Rum Glaze	81
Glossy Chocolate Sauce	81
Lemon Sauce	82

THE SUGAR FIX

Chocolate lovers will go nuts over this rich and creamy dessert. Ice cream or whipped cream complement this beautifully.

Baked Fudge

325⁰   45 – 50 minutes

4 eggs, beaten
2 cups sugar
½ cup flour
½ cup cocoa
½ tsp. salt
½ tsp. cinnamon
1 cup butter, melted
2 tsp. vanilla
1 cup pecans, toasted, chopped

Beat eggs until lemon colored (3-5 minutes). Combine sugar, flour, cocoa, salt, and cinnamon; add to eggs. Mix until well blended. Add butter and vanilla. Stir in pecans. Pour into 9" pie plate, then place into larger pan of hot water. Bake for 45-50 minutes or until center is set. Serve warm with ice cream or sweetened whipped cream.

> Substitute toasted walnuts or almonds for the pecans for a nice variation.

Desserts

We were looking for something different to make at the shop when I got the idea for this cheesecake. We were amazed at how terrific it tasted on the first attempt.

PIÑA COLADA CHEESECAKE

350°   *1 hour*

2 - 8 oz. pkgs. cream cheese, softened
1 cup sugar
3 eggs
½ tsp. salt
2 Tbsp. pineapple juice
½ cup cream of coconut
2 cups sour cream, room temperature
2 tsp. vanilla

Place a large pan in oven that has about ½" water. Allow to heat with oven. Place cream cheese and sugar in large mixer bowl and beat with whip until smooth, approximately 3 minutes. Add eggs, one at a time, mixing well after each. Add salt, cream of coconut, pineapple juice, vanilla, and sour cream. Mix well. Pour into spring form pan with bottom crust and the outside of pan wrapped with double heavy-duty aluminum foil. Bake for 1 hour in pan of water. Turn off oven and allow cake to sit in oven for one more hour. Chill overnight. Remove ring when chilled.

Topping

*20 oz. can crushed pineapple, drained, less 2 Tbsp. for filling
3 Tbsp. starch
1/3 cup sugar
¼ cup rum
Dash salt
1 Tbsp. butter
1 tsp. vanilla
Remaining cream of coconut*

Be sure pineapple is thoroughly drained. Combine sugar and cornstarch in medium, heavy saucepan. Add juice, rum, and salt. Cook on medium until thickened and bubbly; add butter, stir until melted. Allow filling to cool. Add vanilla and cream of coconut. Chill overnight. Spread onto chilled cheesecake and sprinkle with approximately 2 Tbsp. toasted coconut.
This is one of the favored items at the shop. Several customers would not touch a lemon bar with a ten-foot pole. They heard about these, tried them, and then began ordering them by the dozen.

Desserts

Lemon Bars

350⁰   *2/20 minute parts*

2 cups flour   *½ tsp. salt*
½ cup powdered sugar
1 cup butter
2 cups sugar
¼ cup flour
3 eggs
1/3 cup lemon juice
1tsp. lemon extract
2 tsp. vanilla extract
powdered sugar

Combine flour and powdered sugar; cut in butter until crumbly. Press into prepared 9x13" pan and bake for 20 minutes. While crust is baking, mix together sugar, flour, and salt. Add eggs, lemon juice, lemon extract, and vanilla. When crust is done, pour filling over hot crust. Bake for 20 minutes. Allow to cool completely, then dust generously with powdered sugar. Cut into squares; serve cold.

THE SUGAR FIX

My oldest son, Jason, gave me the idea of spreading marshmallow cream over these very moist brownies. We first wanted to call them Swirlies, but decided that wasn't such a good idea.

Marshmallow Whirl Brownies

350⁰   30 minutes

1 cup butter, softened
2 cups sugar
4 oz. semi-sweet chocolate, melted
4 eggs
1 tsp. vanilla
½ tsp. salt
1 ½ cups all purpose flour
½ cup cocoa
1 cup marshmallow cream

By hand, cream butter and sugar. Add melted chocolate; mix until just blended. Add eggs, vanilla, and salt. Mix until just blended. Add flour and cocoa; mix by hand until smooth. Spread into prepared 9X13 pan. In larger container, microwave marshmallow cream for 10 seconds; stir; then spread and swirl over brownies. Bake in pre-heated oven for 30 minutes. Allow to cool approximately 10 minutes before cutting to be able to eat warm brownies.

For plain brownies, leave out marshmallow cream. Pecans or walnuts can be added for a nice crunch.

Desserts

This recipe was developed for the Oklahoma State Sugar Art Show. The show is primarily a cake decorating event, but a tasting event is included. Since the contestant gets free samples of ginger, chocolate, and vanilla, all three must be included in the recipe. That can be a lot harder than it sounds.

Ginger Crunch Bars

350⁰   2/15 minute parts

2 cups oats
1 ¾ cup brown sugar, packed
1 cup flour
½ cup whole wheat flour
½ tsp. baking soda
½ tsp. salt
1 tsp. powdered vanilla
1 cup butter, softened
1 egg1 14 oz. sweetened condensed milk
4 oz. melted chocolate chips
1 tsp. ginger
½ tsp. cinnamon
1 tsp. vanilla
1 cup chopped, toasted pecans
1 cup chocolate chips

In large mixer bowl, mix dry ingredients; add butter and mix until crumbly. Set aside 1¾ cup of the crumb mixture for topping. Add egg to remaining and mix until just blended; spread into bottom prepared 9x13" pan. Bake in preheated oven for 15 minutes. Meanwhile, mix together sweetened condensed milk, melted and cooled chocolate, vanilla bean paste, cinnamon, and ginger puree. Also, mix together reserved topping with pecans, and chopped chocolate. Spread liquid mixture over hot crust, then sprinkle topping evenly over filling. Bake for 15 minutes or until center is set. Allow to cool and cut into bars.

THE SUGAR FIX

While playing with the ginger recipe, I decided to try a version without the extra spices. These are very rich and taste great warm or cool.

Pecan Crunch Bars

350^0 2/15 minute parts

2 cups oats
1 ¾ brown sugar, packed
1 cup flour
½ cup whole wheat flour
1 tsp. baking soda
½ tsp. salt
1 cup butter, softened
1 egg
1–14 oz. can sweetened condensed milk
1 cup chocolate chips, melted
1 tsp. vanilla
1 cup chopped toasted pecans
1 cup chocolate chips

In large mixer bowl, combine dry ingredients; add butter and mix until crumbly. Set aside 1 ¾ cup of the crumb mixture for topping. Add egg to remaining and mix until just blended; spread into bottom of lightly greased and floured 9" x 13" pan. Bake in preheated oven for 15-18 minutes. Meanwhile, mix together sweetened condensed milk, melted and cooled chocolate, and vanilla. Also, mix together reserved topping with pecans and chocolate chips. Spread liquid mixture over slightly cooled crust, then sprinkle topping evenly over filling. Bake for 15 minutes or until center is set. Allow to cool and cut into bars.

Desserts

For those who really like to go the extra mile for their goodies, this caramel sauce is perfect. It's quick, easy, and delicious.

Caramel Sauce

1 cup dark brown sugar
¼ cup corn starch
¼ tsp. salt
1 cup heavy cream
¼ cup light corn syrup
3 Tbsp. butter
2 tsp. vanilla

In a heavy saucepan combine brown sugar, starch, and salt. Stir in cream and corn syrup. Cook and stir over medium heat until thickened and bubbly. Use a whisk to reduce any lumps from the brown sugar. Reduce heat slightly and cook for 2 more minutes. Remove from heat; add butter and vanilla. Serve warm or cool. Store in airtight container in refrigerator once it has come to room temperature.

Do the Gooey Bars (page 98) sound good but you don't have any caramel ice cream topping? Use this. While the crust is cooking, you can make this, then spread it over the crust while it's still hot.

THE SUGAR FIX

I love cheesecake, but sometimes it is too dense. This airy cheesecake melts in your mouth. It's very versatile. You can serve it plain, with cherry, strawberry, or blueberry topping. However you decide to serve it, you will love it.

Cheesecake

350º *1 hour*

2 8-oz. packages cream cheese, softened
2 Tbsp. butter, softened
1 cup sugar
½ tsp. salt
3 eggs
2 tsp. vanilla
3 cups sour cream

Beat cream cheese, butter, sugar, and salt on medium speed until smooth, approximately 3 minutes. Add eggs, one at a time, mixing well after each. Add vanilla and sour cream; mix until just combined. Springform pan should have cookie crust pressed into the bottom. Wrap two layers of heavy-duty aluminum foil around pan. While oven is heating, allow about 1" of water to heat in a larger cake pan. Pour cheesecake mixture into springform pan. Place cheesecake in the pan of hot water. Bake for 1 hour, then turn off oven, leaving cheesecake in the oven for one more hour. Remove from oven, then remove foil. Allow to cool to room temperature, then refrigerate over night. Place on serving plate and top with your choice of topping.

Desserts

My husband thought this cheesecake sounded awful and couldn't understand why so many people ordered it at the shop. Finally he decided to try it and now it's his favorite.

Caramel Pecan Cheesecake

350°   1 hour

2 8-oz. packages cream cheese, softened
2 Tbsp. butter, softened
1 cup sugar
½ tsp. salt
3 eggs
2 tsp. vanilla
3 cups sour cream
1 cup fudge ice cream topping
½ cup chopped toasted pecans
½ cup caramel ice cream topping
Chocolate Cookie Crust

Beat cream cheese, butter, sugar, and salt on medium speed until smooth, approximately 3 minutes. Add eggs, one at a time, mixing well after each. Add vanilla and sour cream; mix until just combined. Springform pan should have Chocolate Cookie Crust (page 48) pressed into the bottom. Wrap two layers of heavy-duty aluminum foil around pan. While oven is heating, allow about 1" of water to heat in a larger cake pan. Pour cheesecake mixture into springform pan. Place cheesecake in the pan of hot water. Bake for 1 hour, then turn off oven, leaving cheesecake in the oven for one more hour. Remove from oven, then remove foil. Allow to cool to room temperature, then refrigerate over night. Place on serving plate. Spread slightly warmed fudge topping over cake, sprinkle with pecans, then drizzle slightly warmed caramel over cake.

THE SUGAR FIX

When trying to come up with an entry for the local chocolate festival, I remembered how great chocolate and caramel are together. When I made this, it was so well received that I sold three whole cakes (instead of the normal piece of cake) in 15 minutes. It's call Chocolate Earthquake because it was still too warm to serve and it cracked down the middle. No one cared, they wanted it boxed up to take home even if it was falling apart. By the way, I won first place at the festival.

Chocolate Earthquake

1 – 8" round layer of The Best Chocolate Cake (page 6)

½ recipe of Caramel Pie Filling (page 65)

¼ cup toasted chopped pecans.

½ recipe of Chocolate Sheet Cake Frosting (page 38)

Split or torte cake in half, remove top and reserve. Stir pecans into slightly warmed pie filling. Spread filling evenly over bottom half of cake. Replace top then spread warm Chocolate Sheet Cake Frosting over the top allowing some to drip down side. To serve warm, place 1 serving on microwave safe plate and warm 30 seconds on medium power.

If you make the full recipes listed above, triple wrap the other half of the cake in plastic wrap and the filling/frosting in plastic containers. Allow cake to come to room temperature before unwrapping and do not over heat frosting or filling. Then you have a quick and delicious dessert ready and waiting.

Desserts

Fruit crisps are always a favorite quick dessert. Ice cream or fresh whipped cream add even more flavor.

Apple Crisp

350°   45 minutes

½ cup rolled oats
½ cup dark brown sugar, packed
¼ cup all-purpose flour
1 tsp. cinnamon
½ tsp. allspice
¼ tsp. salt
¼ cup butter
6 medium tart apples
¼ cup sugar
½ tsp. cinnamon
1 tsp. vanilla

Combine oats, brown sugar, flour, cinnamon, allspice, and salt. Cut in butter until crumbly. Set aside. Peel, core, and thinly slice apples. In large bowl coat apples with a mixture of cinnamon, sugar, and vanilla. Pour into 10" x 10" square glass baking dish. Sprinkle crumb mixture evenly over apples. Bake for 45 minutes.

THE SUGAR FIX

This cake was favored by a judge for his restaurant, but was considered too time consuming for the regular baker.

Creamy Chocolate Torte

1 recipe "The Best Chocolate Cake "(page 6), made into 8" rounds.

1 recipe "Chocolate Italian Buttercream" (page 50)

Chocolate Sauce

¼ cup butter
½ cup heavy cream
1 cup sugar
2 ounces pre-melted chocolate
2 tsp. vanilla

Combine all ingredients, except vanilla in heavy saucepan. Cook over medium heat it begins to thicken and bubble. Continue to cook for 1 minute. Remove from heat and add vanilla. Allow to cool to luke warm, stirring occasionally.

Split cake layers. Place first layer on cake plate, poke holes with skewer, then spread about 1/3 cup chocolate sauce over layer. Spread Italian Buttercream on layer, bringing to edges. Repeat with two of the remaining layers. Place top layer on cake then frost entire cake with Italian Buttercream. Sprinkle toasted, chopped pecans on top of cake. Can be served at room temperature, but must be stored in the refrigerator.

Desserts

The two following recipes were more experiments for the tasting division of the Sugar Art Show. They were made to go on the cake, but are just as great on ice cream.

Orange Rum Glaze

½ cup sugar
2 Tbsp. Corn starch
Juice of one medium orange, strained.
½ tsp. Orange zest
Water to make 1 cup of juice and water
¼ cup Rum
1 Tbsp. Butter
1 tsp. Vanilla

In small saucepan, stir together sugar, starch, and salt. Add juice and water mixture, zest, and rum. Cook on medium heat until bubbly, stirring constantly. Add butter and vanilla; stir. Pour approximately half over warm cake or ice cream. Reserve remaining for serving with cake.

Glossy Chocolate Sauce

¾ cup clear corn syrup
3 oz. Semi sweet chocolate, chopped
1 Tbsp. Butter
1 tsp. Vanilla

In microwave safe container, heat corn syrup and chocolate for 1 minute on high. Stir to melt chocolate. Add remaining ingredients. Use whisk to thoroughly mix chocolate. Drizzle over cooled cake or over ice cream.

THE SUGAR FIX

Pour this over the Lemon Pound Cake (page 30), Buttermilk Pound Cake (page27), or as a filling for the Lemonade Cake (page 20). It could also be served chilled in tart shells.

Lemon Sauce

½ cup sugar
2 Tbsp. corn starch
dash salt
¼ cup freshly squeezed lemon juice
¼ tsp. lemon zest
¾ cup water
1 Tbsp. butter
1 tsp. lemon extract
1 tsp. Vanilla

In small saucepan, stir together sugar, starch, and salt. Add juice, zest, and water. Cook and stir over medium heat until bubbly. Reduce heat to medium low and cook and additional 2 minutes. Add butter, lemon extract, and vanilla; stir. Sauce can be served warm or cold.

Cookies

Snickerdoodles 84
Chocolate Chip Cookies 85
Desert Cookies 86
Chocolate Peanut Butter Chip Cookies 87
Oatmeal Cookies 88
Crispy Crunchy Chocolate Chip Cookies 89
Sugar Cookies 90
Triple Chippers 91
Cut Out Cookie Dough 92
Brown Sugar Cut Out Cookies 94
Chocolate Cut Out Cookies 95
Gooey Bars 96
Peanut Butter Cookies 97
Peanut Butter Chocolate Chip Cookies 97

THE SUGAR FIX

When **"The Sugar Fix"** first opened, I wanted to make Snickerdoodles, but didn't have any of the cream of tartar that is normally used in these cookies. I decided to try buttermilk instead. They turned out better than expected, so I adjusted the recipe to fit the new ingredient. I like a lot of cinnamon on the cookies, so I make the sugar with double cinnamon. If you like them lighter, just use one teaspoon of cinnamon.

Snickerdoodles

375^0 11 minutes

1 cup butter, softened
2 cups sugar
2 eggs
2 tsp. vanilla
1/3 cup buttermilk
4 cups flour
½ tsp. baking soda
½ tsp. salt
½ cup sugar
1-2 tsp. cinnamon

Cream butter and 2 cups sugar until light and fluffy. Add eggs and vanilla; mix until just combined. Add buttermilk. Sift together flour, baking soda, and salt. Add to butter mixture. mix until just combined. Mix together remaining ½ cup sugar and cinnamon. Form dough into 1" balls and roll in cinnamon/sugar mix. Place about 2" apart on lightly greased or parchment lined cookie sheets. Bake for 11 minutes. Centers will be slightly soft.

Every time I offer to make cookies at home, the boys immediately ask for these. Kyle doesn't like pecans; so I make one pan without, then add them for the rest of us.

Chocolate Chip Cookies

375^0 11 minutes

1 cup butter, softened
1 ½ cups packed, dark brown sugar
2 eggs
2 tsp. vanilla
3 cups all-purpose flour
1 tsp. baking soda
½ tsp. salt
1 cup mini chocolate chips
½ cup toasted, chopped pecans

Cream butter and brown sugar until light and fluffy. Add eggs and vanilla. Stir together flour, baking soda, and salt; add to butter mixture. Beat slowly until just combined. Stir in chocolate chips and pecans. Place 1" balls of dough about 2" apart on lightly greased or parchment lined cookie sheet. Bake for 11 minutes or until centers are just set.

One of my favorite tools for cookies is a 1" diameter ice cream type scoop. They come in other sizes as well and make cookie making very quick and easy.

THE SUGAR FIX

When my son, Kyle was 7 years old, he kept asking me to make desert cookies. I told him I had never heard of them and would need a recipe. After having this conversation several times, he came up with the recipe on his own. We only had to adjust the amount of baking soda to make these wonderful cinnamon cookies.

Desert Cookies

375^0 11 minutes

1 cup butter, softened
2 cups sugar
2 eggs
2 tsp. vanilla
3 cups flour
½ tsp. baking soda
½ tsp. salt
2 tsp. cinnamon
Mix: ½ cup sugar & 1 tsp. cinnamon.

Cream butter and sugar. Beat on medium for 1 minute. Add eggs, one at a time. Add vanilla. Combine flour, soda, and salt. Add to butter mixture along with cinnamon. Mix until just combined. Make 1" balls and roll in cinnamon/sugar mix. Place on lightly greased cookie sheet approximately 2" apart. Bake on parchment line cookie sheet for 11 minutes.

> Kyle called them desert cookies because they are the color of sand.

Cookies

I love to play with recipes and my family agrees. When I made these cookies during a family game night, there were none left by the end of the night.

Chocolate Peanut Butter Chip Cookies

375⁰   *11 minutes*

1 cup butter, softened
1 ½ cups packed, dark brown sugar
½ cup chocolate chips, melted and cooled
2 eggs
2 tsp. vanilla
3 cups all-purpose flour
1 tsp. baking soda
½ tsp. salt
1 cup peanut butter chips

Cream butter and brown sugar until light and fluffy. Add melted chocolate, eggs, and vanilla. Stir together flour, baking soda, and salt; add to butter mixture. Beat slowly until just combined. Stir in peanut butter chips. Place 1" balls of dough about 2" apart on lightly greased or parchment lined cookie sheet. Bake for 11 minutes or until centers are just set.

Use a glass measuring cup to melt chocolate chips. Heat in the microwave on high for one minute, then stir until smooth.

THE SUGAR FIX

My mom gave the basis for this recipe when I opened **"The Sugar Fix"**. I made a few minor changes, including the newly available cinnamon chips.

Oatmeal Cookies

375^0 11 minutes

1 cup butter
1 cup brown sugar
1 cup sugar
2 eggs
2 tsp. vanilla
2 cups flour
1 tsp. baking powder
¼ tsp. baking soda
½ tsp. cinnamon
¼ tsp. allspice
¼ tsp. cloves
¼ tsp. ginger
½ tsp. salt
3 cups rolled oats
1 cup cinnamon chips
1 cup chopped pecans
½ cup raisins (optional

Cream butter and sugars. Add eggs and vanilla. Mix together dry ingredients; add to butter mixture; mix until just blended. Stir in pecans and cinnamon chips (and raisins). Drop by spoonfuls (approximately 1" in diameter) onto lightly greased or parchment lined cookie sheet. Bake for 11 minutes. Centers will be slightly soft.

These cookies went like hot cakes at the shop. I was given the basic recipe, but changed it quite a bit to suit my own tastes. The dough looks odd and thin, but the cookies come out beautifully.

Crispy Crunchy Chocolate Chip Cookies

350⁰   17 minutes

1 cup butter, softened
1 cup sugar
1 cup dark brown sugar
2 eggs
1 cup peanut oil*
2 tsp. vanilla
3 cups flour
1 tsp. salt
1 tsp. baking soda
1 cup mini-chocolate chips
1 cup rolled oats
1 cup rice cereal
½ cup toasted, chopped pecans

Cream butter, sugar, and brown sugar. Add eggs, peanut oil, and vanilla; mix well. Stir together flour, salt, and baking soda. Add to butter mixture; mix on low until just combined. Stir in chocolate chips, then oats, then cereal, and pecans. Do not try to stir everything at the same time. Spoon 1" balls onto parchment lined cookie sheet. Bake for 17 minutes or until centers are just set. Edges will be brown while the centers are very light brown.

*For those with peanut allergies, use a good quality cooking oil instead.

If you like raisins, try adding a half cup after stirring in the nuts and cereal.

THE SUGAR FIX

These are the lightest, crispest, melt in your mouth cookies. It's almost impossible to no less than five or six.

Sugar Cookies

350⁰   8 minutes

1 cup butter, softened
1 cup sugar
1 egg
1 tsp. almond extract
1 tsp. vanilla
2 cups flour
2 tsp. baking powder
½ tsp. salt
(½ cup sugar in small bowl)

Cream butter and sugar until fluffy. Add egg, vanilla, and almond extracts. Combine dry ingredients, then add to butter mixture. Form dough into 1" balls, then roll in ½ cup sugar. Place on lightly greased or parchment lined cookie sheets, then press with bottom of sugar coated glass. Bake for 8 minutes or until edges are barely golden. Cool on wire rack. These cookies are very delicate and must be handled gently.

These are fun cookies for chocolate lovers, and a little bit of a change from traditional chocolate chip cookies.

Triple Chippers

375°   11 minutes

1 cup butter, softened
1 cup brown sugar, packed
½ cup sugar
2 eggs
2 tsp. vanilla
3 cups all-purpose flour
1 tsp. baking soda
½ tsp. salt
1 cup semi-sweet chocolate chips
1 cup milk chocolate chips
1 cup white chocolate chips

Cream butter and sugars until fluffy. Add eggs and vanilla; mix well. Stir together flour, baking soda, and salt. Add to butter mixture, mix until just combined. Stir in chips, one type at a time to ensure even distribution. Drop 1" balls onto parchment lined or lightly greased cookie sheets. Bake for 11 minutes.

Pecans or walnuts are a very nice addition to these cookies.

THE SUGAR FIX

When I make decorated cookies, I like them very thin and this recipe is delicious with or without frosting. You can roll them thicker if you like, cook them the same amount of time, and they will still be soft.

Cut Out Cookie Dough

375^0 11 minutes

1 cup butter, softened
2 cups sugar
2 eggs
1 tsp. almond extract
2 tsp. vanilla extract
5 cups flour
1 ½ tsp. baking powder
¼ tsp. baking soda
1 tsp. salt
1/3 cup buttermilk

Cream butter and sugar, beat until fluffy. Add eggs, one at a time, mixing well after each. Add extracts. Combine flour, baking powder, baking soda, and salt; mix alternately with buttermilk. Roll about 1/6 of the dough between two sheets of parchment paper or waxed paper to approximately 1/16th of an inch. Place on cookie sheet, then in freezer until firm. Roll out remaining dough in the same manner. When dough is firm (approximately 30 minutes), working with one sheet at a time, peel off parchment paper from both sides. Allow dough to remain on one of the loose sheets. Cut cookies quickly and place 2 inches apart on lightly greased or parchment lined cookie sheets. Bake at 375F for 11 minutes. Allow to cool completely before decorating with royal or buttercream frosting. Without frosting, cookies will be light and crisp. With frosting, cookies will be soft.

Cookies

Cookie Bouquet

This made a lot of people really happy to receive for Christmas. Each cookie, including the ones in the jar, is individually decorated. There's that obsessive-compulsive behavior again!

THE SUGAR FIX

Try something different with your cut out cookies. Dipped in white chocolate, milk chocolate, or dark chocolate, these cookies are not only delicious but beautiful as well.

Brown Sugar Cut Out Cookies

350^0 11 minutes

1 cup butter, softened
1 ½ cups dark brown sugar, packed
1 egg
2 tsp. vanilla
3 cups all-purpose flour
½ tsp. baking soda
½ tsp. salt

Cream butter and brown sugar, beat until light and fluffy; about 2 minutes. Add egg and vanilla; beat until just combined. Stir together flour, baking soda, and salt. Add to butter mixture; mix until just combined. Divide dough into fourths, then roll each section between two sheets of parchment paper. Use dowel rods (1/16" to 1/8") on each side to be sure the dough is evenly rolled. Place on cookie sheet and then in freezer for about 20 minutes. Peel away parchment from one side, lay it back on top, flip the rolled out dough and remove the parchment paper. Quickly cut desired shapes and place them on a cookie sheet that has been lightly greased or lined with parchment paper. Bake for 11 minutes; allow cookies to cool completely before removing from parchment paper. Decorate with melted chocolate or Royal Icing (page 53).

Chocolate Cut Out Cookies

350⁰   11 minutes

1 cup butter, softened
1 ¾ cup powdered sugar
1 egg
2 tsp. vanilla
1 tsp. almond extract
2 ½ cups all-purpose flour
½ cup cocoa, sifted
¼ tsp. baking soda
½ tsp. salt

Beat butter and powdered sugar until light and fluffy. Add egg, vanilla, and almond extract; beat until just combined. Stir together flour, cocoa, baking soda, and salt. Add to butter mixture; beat until just combined. Divide dough into fourths, then roll each section between two sheets of parchment paper. Use dowel rods (1/16" to 1/8") on each side to be sure the dough is evenly rolled. Place on cookie sheet and then in freezer for about 20 minutes. Peel away parchment from one side, lay it back on top, flip the rolled out dough and remove the parchment paper. Quickly cut desired shapes and place them on a cookie sheet that has been lightly greased or lined with parchment paper. Bake for 11 minutes; allow cookies to cool completely before removing from parchment paper. Decorate with melted chocolate or Royal Icing (page 53).

> Since the dough is not being rolled out with flour, the scraps can be re-rolled without becoming tough. The chocolate, brown sugar and vanilla cookie doughs can be kneaded together to make marbled cookies.
> Leftovers can be frozen if properly wrapped in plastic wrap. Allow to come to room temperature before trying to roll out leftover dough.

THE SUGAR FIX

When I started making these at **"The Sugar Fix"**, they sold out during the first lunch rush. The high school students were buying several at a time. They are unbelievably good warm and still delicious at room temperature. Use the best caramel topping you can find.

Gooey Bars

350⁰   25 minutes

1 cup butter
1 ½ cups dark brown sugar, packed
2 ½ cups all-purpose flour
1 tsp. baking soda
½ tsp. salt
2 tsp. vanilla
3 cups rolled oats
2 eggs
1 cup caramel ice cream topping
1 cup mini-chocolate chips, divided
½ cup toasted pecans, chopped, divided

Cream butter and sugar, beat until fluffy. Add flour, baking soda, salt vanilla, and oats. Beat until crumbly. Reserve about 3 cups for the topping. Add eggs to oat mixture; beat until just combined. Press dough into bottom of prepared 9"x13" pan. Spread slightly warmed caramel over crust. Sprinkle half of the chocolate chips and half of the pecans over caramel. Sprinkle the reserved topping over the caramel, then the remaining chocolate chips and pecans. Press lightly to set. Bake for 25 minutes or until center is set. Let cool 15 minutes before cutting into bars.

I prefer to use the mini chocolate chips because they distribute the flavor more evenly. Regular or large chocolate chips can be used also.

Cookies

When I ask my husband what kind of cookies he would like, he immediately says "peanut butter". The secret to really great cookies is to use old-fashioned peanut butter. Pour off the oil from the top before measuring the quantity you need. You can put the oil back in the jar to prevent the peanut butter drying out.

Peanut Butter Cookies

375^0 11 minutes

1 cup butter, softened
1 cup peanut butter
2 cups dark brown sugar, packed
2 eggs
2 tsp. vanilla
3 cups flour
1 tsp. baking soda
½ tsp. salt
½ cup sugar

In large mixer bowl, cream butter, peanut butter, and brown sugar. Beat until fluffy. Add eggs and vanilla. Stir together flour, baking soda, and salt. Add to butter mixture, mix until just blended. Form 1" balls, roll in the ½ cup sugar and place on parchment lined cookie sheet approximately 2" apart. Press criss-cross pattern into cookies with tines of a dinner fork. Bake for 11 minutes.

Peanut Butter Chocolate Chip Cookies

Stir 1 cup chocolate chips into dough before forming into balls. Continue following instructions.

A message from the author.

Since we can't and shouldn't always have dessert, I have included some recipes that my family loves and some that were very popular at **"The Sugarfix"**. So the next two sections are a compilation of favorites and "good to know" recipes.

There are also a few recipes for the sugar artist. For these recipes, you might have to go to a cake decorating store for some of the supplies or they can be ordered online through cake decorating suppliers. Prices will vary from vendor to vendor. Quality can also vary. For the sugar artist, there is a LOT of experimenting involved and it not always the cheapest hobby to have. Anyone interested in sugar art should check their area and the Internet for any local cake shows and cake club meetings. It's amazing what can be done with a lump of what appears to be play dough. At these shows and meetings a person can learn skills and of classes that are being offered by sugar artists from around the world. Many of these artists travel the United States giving classes for 2 to 5 days. These classes are not cheap, but what can be learned is invaluable. The classes are also a great deal of fun. Some of the cake designers that I know really loosen up during a class. The combination of the intensity of the class, the sometimes late hours, and the variety of personalities can make just about anyone a little "loopy". ☺ Most of the designers that take these classes consider them a working vacation. BEWARE! Once you take one of these classes, you're hooked!

Dinners

Chicken & Dumplings	100
Beef Stew	101
Tortilla Soup	102
Italian Sausage Stew	103
Garlic Chicken & Rice	104
Perfectly Easy Roast	105
Gravy	105
Garlic Chicken Soup	106
Lasagna	107
Sausage Bread	108
Taco Pie	109
Chicken & Rice	110
Onion Burgers	111
No Effort BBQ	112

THE SUGAR FIX

When I made this at "The Sugar Fix", there was never enough. I started with about 6 quarts the first time and quickly made up to 20 quarts. I still ran out. People even called to find out when I was planning to make them again. I did not make the same thing every day of the week. I enjoyed making what I wanted. Eventually, I had to at least plan for the week so my customers would know when I was making their favorite.

Chicken & Dumplings

1 whole 3-4 lb. chicken, washed
1 large can chicken broth
4 cups water
3 cups all purpose flour
1 tsp. salt
1 tsp. black pepper
3 Tbsp. shortening
½ cup milk

Salt and pepper chicken to taste. Bake covered, in 375° oven for 1 hour, then uncovered for 30 minutes. Remove from pan, strain drippings into heatproof cup, refrigerate. Allow chicken to cool enough to handle. Remove meat from bone and cut into bite size pieces, refrigerate. In large stockpot heat chicken broth and water to boiling, add salt and pepper to taste. Remove fat from reserved drippings and add remaining gelatinous broth to boiling broth. Stir together flour, salt, and pepper. Cut in shortening with pastry blender. Stir in milk a little at a time until dough is slightly sticky. Divide into thirds. Roll 1/3 out very thinly on floured surface. Cut into bite sized pieces. Drop pieces into boiling broth, stir. Repeat with remaining dough. Bring to boil then add chicken. Cook on medium heat until broth is slightly thick.

Use a pizza cutting wheel to make cutting the dumplings faster and easier.

Even my kids, who hate stew, would eat this. It's a very simple stew that you can add vegetables to suit your own tastes.

Beef Stew

2-lbs. chuck roast, cubed, fat removed
3 Tbsp. olive oil
¼ cup finely chopped onion
3 cloves garlic, crushed
1 cup baby carrots, coarsely chopped
3-4 medium potatoes, peeled and cubed
4 cups beef broth
3 cups water
salt and pepper to taste
¼ cup flour
1 cup water

In large skillet, heat olive oil, and then sauté chuck roast, onions, garlic, carrots, and potatoes until beef is just browned. Add a small amount of salt and pepper during cooking. Meanwhile, heat broth and water to a gentle boil. Add beef mixture; simmer 30 minutes. Mix the flour and 1 cup water together until smooth. Add to stew through strainer. Continue simmering until thickened, about 15 minutes.

Using a plastic bag with about 1 cup of flour to coat the meat will add a little extra flavor and color. Remove meat from flour before sautéing.

THE SUGAR FIX

When someone likes spicy, they love this soup. It is terrific for a cold winter's day. Of course, you can adjust the amount of heat to your particular taste.

Tortilla Soup

2 Tbsp. butter
2 Tbsp. olive oil
1 medium onion, chopped
1 cup baby carrots, coarsely chopped
2 celery ribs, chopped
2-3 chicken breasts, diced
4 10.5 oz cans chicken broth
1 26.5 oz. can spaghetti sauce
2 tsp. red pepper sauce
1 tsp. ground cumin
2 Tbsp. chili powder
1 tsp. salt
1 tsp. lemon pepper
1 tsp. black pepper
¼ cup jalapeno slices
6 corn tortillas cut into strips

Heat butter and olive oil in large skillet over medium high heat. Sauté onion, carrots, and chicken. Cook until chicken is just turning brown. Meanwhile, in large stock pot, heat chicken broth, spaghetti sauce, red pepper sauce, cumin, chili powder, salt, lemon pepper, and black pepper. When hot, add chicken mixture and jalapeno slices. Allow to simmer 30 minutes. Quick fry tortilla strips in about ½ cup cooking oil until crisp. Drain on paper toweling. Garnish bowls with tortilla strips.

This stew will warm up just about any cold day. It can be made and served within the hour or can cooking in a crock-pot all day. If you decide to use the crock-pot, be sure to cut the potatoes a little larger and use the lowest setting.

Italian Sausage Stew

2 Tbsp. olive oil
1 Tbsp. butter
2 lbs. Italian sausage links, cut to bite size pieces
1 small red onion, chopped
4 cloves garlic, minced
1 tsp. salt
1 tsp. fresh black pepper
3-4 medium potatoes, peeled and cubed
4 cups chicken broth
1 – 26 oz. can spaghetti sauce
2 tsp. oregano
1 green bell pepper, cored, seeded, and diced
1 jalapeno, seeded, and chopped (optional)

Heat large skillet to very hot; add olive oil, butter, sausage, onion, garlic, salt, and pepper. Cook on medium-high heat until sausage is almost done; add potatoes. Cook until potatoes are barely browned, but not completely cooked. Meanwhile, heat chicken broth in stockpot to a gentle boil. When sausage is done, add to chicken broth along with spaghetti sauce, oregano, bell pepper, and jalapeno (optional). Cook on medium until potatoes are done.

THE SUGAR FIX

My family eats a lot of chicken, so I wanted something new and different that didn't require a lot of effort. This is a new family favorite.

Garlic Chicken & Rice

3-4 skinless, boneless chicken breasts
3 Tbsp. olive oil
1 medium red onion, chopped
6 cloves garlic, sliced
salt & pepper to taste
2-14 oz. cans chicken broth
4 Tbsp. butter, divided
¼ cup lemon juice

Cut chicken breasts into bite size pieces. Heat large skillet over medium high heat; add olive oil, chicken, half of the onion and garlic, and salt & pepper. Sauté until chicken is golden brown. While chicken is cooking, heat lemon juice until reduced by half. Add broth and simmer until reduced by half. Add lemon juice and 2 Tbsp. butter; continue cooking until butter is melted. Prepare either instant rice or uncooked rice according to package directions. The addition of salt, pepper, and the remaining butter will make the two parts of the meal blend well. Serve chicken over rice with a generous amount of sauce.

Dinners

For busy people, this is a perfect start to an easy dinner. By following these directions, the roast will be well done, but very tender. I suppose if you like your roast a little less done use the low setting of the crock-pot. Since my family likes our meat well done, I really don't know how it will work out at a lower temperature. Serve with mashed potatoes or add cut potatoes to pot during the last hour for an oven-roasted taste.

Perfectly Easy Roast

3-4 pound roast of your choice, <u>frozen</u>
1 medium onion, sliced
2 cloves garlic, crushed or sliced
salt & pepper to taste.

Spray crock-pot with vegetable spray. Place <u>frozen</u> roast in crock-pot. Cover roast with remaining ingredients. DO NOT ADD WATER. Cover and cook on high for 6-8 hours. Remove from pot; let stand 5-10 minutes before slicing. Meanwhile, strain juices into small saucepan to make gravy.

Gravy

Roast drippings
½ cup cold water
2 Tbsp. corn starch
salt & pepper to taste.

Heat roast drippings on medium heat to a gentle boil. Mix water and corn starch in separate container until starch is dissolved. Add to drippings along with salt and pepper. Stir until thickened and bubbly.

For lower fat, strain roast drippings into a grease separator cup before adding to the saucepan.

THE SUGAR FIX

When my soups were becoming a bit hit at the shop, I really wanted something different, but was drawing a blank. Then from out of the blue came this recipe. It was an immediate hit. It has a very large amount of garlic, but the taste is mellow and soothing.

Garlic Chicken Soup

2 – 3 chicken breasts
2 Tbsp. olive oil
1 full garlic head, peeled
¼ cup chopped red onion
salt & pepper to taste
2 Tbsp. butter
6 cups chicken broth
3 cups water
2 cups dry penne pasta

Cut chicken breast into bite sized pieces. Heat large skillet on medium high heat add olive oil, chicken, onion, salt and pepper. Put garlic through press and add to skillet. Cook until chicken is golden brown; stirring occasionally. Add butter and stir until melted. Meanwhile, in stockpot, heat broth and water to almost boiling. Add chicken and pasta. Cook on medium heat until pasta is al dente. Serve hot.

I didn't realize that my family hated the ricotta cheese in lasagna until I forgot to get some at the store. This recipe still has a lot of cheese and is a little easier to make.

Lasagna

350º   *1 hour*

2 Tbsp. olive oil
2 lbs. lean hamburger
1 pound sausage
salt & pepper to taste
1 26.5 oz. can spaghetti sauce
6 pieces ready-to-use lasagna pasta
1 lb. grated Colby/Jack cheese
1 lb. provolone cheese
1 lb. mozzarella cheese
½ cup parmesan cheese

Using a large skillet, brown hamburger and sausage in olive oil; drain if necessary. Add salt and pepper during cooking. Stir in spaghetti sauce; cook until liquid is absorbed by the meat. Place 3 pieces of pasta in bottom of lasagna pan. Layer half of the meat, then half of the cheeses on pasta. Place the last 3 pieces of pasta over cheese. Layer the remaining meat and cheeses. Cover with foil. Bake for 45 minutes; remove foil, bake an additional 15 minutes. Allow to cool 10 minutes before serving.

If you do like ricotta, mix 1 pound ricotta cheese with one egg, then spread on top of lasagna pasta, before the meat sauce.

THE SUGAR FIX

My family loves this recipe, especially when I use spicy sausage. It tastes great hot or cold. It works great for buffet style dinners. Make some ahead of time, wrap well in aluminum foil, and then freeze. After thawing, warm in 170 degree oven for about 20 minutes until warm, then cut into 1" slices.

Sausage Bread

1 cup buttermilk, 105F
3 Tbsp. butter, softened
1 egg
3 ½ cups flour
2 Tbsp. sugar
1 tsp. salt
1 tsp. yeast
½ lb. sausage
¾ cup grated Colby jack cheese
melted butter

Place buttermilk, butter, egg, flour, sugar, salt, and yeast in bread machine pan. Set bread maker to dough. When dough is ready, begin cooking sausage, crumbled. Cut piece of parchment paper or waxed paper to fit cookie sheet. Roll dough to fit in this area, 1 inch from the edges. Press grease out of sausage with paper toweling. Sprinkle liberally over dough, leaving and edge for sealing. Sprinkle with cheese. Roll up dough to make a loaf, seal edges. Brush with melted butter. Let rise to about double (30 minutes). Bake at 375° for 20 minutes or until crust is golden. Cut into one inch slices; serve hot or cold.

Dinners

My family loves this recipe and it is often requested for a special birthday meal. For those who don't like or can't take spicy, just leave out the salsa and use mild taco seasoning mix.

Taco Pie

1 – 10" pie shell, baked
1 small can refried beans (optional)
¼ cup salsa
1 lb. Hamburger
1 lb. sausage
1 pkg. taco seasoning mix
1 can beef broth
tortilla chips
1 ½ lbs. grated Colby/Jack cheese

Brown hamburger and sausage; drain excess fat. Add seasoning and beef broth. Bring to boil, then simmer until most of the liquid is gone. Mix together refried beans and salsa; spread half into bottom of pie shell. Layer half of the seasoned meat, cheese, & chips. Add remaining refried beans, then meat and top with cheese. Bake in 350° oven for 20 minutes or until cheese is bubbly. Let stand a few minutes before serving.

If you dislike refried beans, but like the salsa, mix the salsa with the meat and leave out the beans.

THE SUGAR FIX

When you want something really satisfying and filling, this fits the bill. It takes a little time to make, but the results are astounding.

Chicken & Rice

1- 10 ¾ oz. can cream of chicken soup
1- 14 oz. can chicken broth
1 cup rice (instant is better, but regular rice will work also)
1 stick butter
½ cup flour
½ cup Parmesan cheese
1 tsp. paprika
salt & pepper to taste
4 – 5 boneless, skinless chicken breasts

Mix together first three ingredients and pour into lasagna pan. Melt butter in medium bowl and set aside. Mix dry ingredients together. Dip chicken into melted butter, then into flour mixture; coating both sides. Place chicken on top of rice. Bake at 350° for 1 hour.

My kids went from just enjoying hamburgers to begging for these. The onions really keep them juicy and full of flavor.

Onion Burgers

6 burgers
1 medium onion, thinly sliced
2-3 garlic cloves, thinly sliced
1 ½ lbs. lean hamburger
olive oil
salt and pepper to taste

In large skillet sauté on medium-high heat onions and garlic in about 2 Tbsp. olive oil until onions start to soften, stirring often. Meanwhile, form hamburger patties, brush with olive oil, then salt and pepper to taste. Remove onions and garlic to a small bowl. Add hamburger patties to hot pan. Place onions and garlic over burgers. Reduce heat slightly. Cook about 5 minutes. Move onions off burgers, then turn over. Replace onions. Continue cooking to desired doneness. Serve on toasted buns.

To easily make hamburgers the same size, use a half-cup measuring cup to lightly pack hamburger before forming into patties.

THE SUGAR FIX

Because I am so picky about what I eat, I am extremely careful about removing any fat that may be on any meat. Some of my customers would not eat a BBQ sandwich because they had the same thought fat in a sandwich. I talked them into trying mine and won over another customer.

No Effort BBQ

> 3-4 lbs. chuck roast, shoulder roast, or brisket - frozen
> salt and pepper to taste
> 2 cups BBQ Sauce

Place frozen meat into crock-pot, sprinkle with salt and pepper. Pour BBQ sauce over meat. Cover and let cook 8-10 hours on the low setting. Remove from crock-pot onto cutting board that has been placed inside of a cookie sheet. Allow to cool slightly. Chop meat into small pieces; place in a serving bowl. Add some of the broth from the crock pot and some extra BBQ sauce over meat and stir. Warm in microwave for 1 minute on high.

> For a party or church social, discard drippings from crock-pot and put the BBQ back into it. Keep the heat on low, stirring occasionally.

Miscellaneous Recipes

Pan Coating 114
Banana Nut Bread 115
Buttermilk Biscuits 116
Ice Box Rolls 117
Pumpkin Bread 118
Bread Machine Bread 119
Light Wheat 119
Gumpaste 121
Gum Glue 123
Pastillage 124
Chocolate Leather 126

THE SUGAR FIX

This is the simplest and most effective way to prevent cakes from sticking to the pan. It is so easy to use and store. All you need is an airtight container that is large enough to store a pastry brush with it. I prefer a plastic brush because they don't lose their bristles as easily.

Pan Coating

    1 cup shortening
    1 cup flour
    1 cup cooking oil

Blend shortening and flour slowly until smooth; add oil. Continue beating until very smooth and creamy. Brush evenly into baking pans to prevent sticking. Store in pantry or shelves.

This recipe can be made in very large batches for the prolific baker. Just be sure to use the same ratios.

Miscellaneous Recipes

Banana Nut Bread is always a favorite any time of the year. This one is moist, easy, and delicious. I hope you enjoy it.

Banana Nut Bread

350° 60 minutes

*3 cups all purpose flour
1 ½ cups sugar
1 ½ tsp. baking powder
½ tsp. baking soda
½ tsp. salt
½ cup butter, softened
1 cup ripe, mashed banana
1 cup buttermilk
2 eggs
2 tsp. vanilla
1 cup chopped, toasted pecans*

In large mixer bowl, combine flour, sugar, baking powder, baking soda, and salt. Add butter and banana, beat on low speed until just combined. Mix together buttermilk, eggs, and vanilla. Add to mixture, blend well. Stir in pecans. Pour into 2 prepared loaf pans. Bake for 1 hour or until skewer comes out clean. Cool 10 minutes, then turn out onto wire rack to cool completely. Turn right side up to prevent breaking from the hump on top of the bread. Serve warm or cool.

THE SUGAR FIX

This is another recipe developed by my mother. I don't think I've changed anything, but this is the way I've been making them for a long time. My oldest son, Jason, loves them so much that I make a batch and a half, so that he can have several for breakfast.

Buttermilk Biscuits

500° 12 minutes

2 cups all-purpose flour
1 Tbsp. baking powder
½ tsp. baking soda
½ tsp. salt
2 Tbsp. shortening
1 ¼ cups buttermilk
2 Tbsp. shortening

Sift together flour, baking powder, baking soda, and salt. Cut in shortening with pastry cutter. Add buttermilk; stir until just combined. Turn out onto floured surface. Dust a small amount of flour on dough, then fold over itself 10 times. Flatten by hand to about ½" thick. Place 2 Tbsp. shortening into heavy glass square baking dish, put into hot oven to allow shortening to melt. Cut with 3-inch diameter biscuit cutter. When shortening is melted, carefully dip biscuits in shortening, then turn over so that both sides have shortening on them. Bake for 12 minutes or until bottom is a golden brown. Serve hot with butter and honey.

> The high temperature allows the dough to rise quickly for light and airy biscuits.

Miscellaneous Recipes

This makes a very large batch of rolls. It's perfect for holidays or to have fresh rolls several days in a row.

Ice Box Rolls

400⁰   17 minutes

1 cup butter, softened
½ cup sugar
1 ½ tsp. salt
1 cup boiling milk
3 eggs, beaten
1 cup luke warm water, divided
2 pkg. active dry yeast
7 ½ cups flour
Melted butter

In medium sized bowl combine butter, sugar, and salt. Beat until smooth with wooden spoon. Add boiling milk; stir. Cool to luke warm. In very large bowl sprinkle yeast over ½ cup warm water, dissolve. Add butter mixture and eggs; mix well. Add flour alternately with remaining water; beat until smooth. Grease dough, cover and place in refrigerator over night. Divide dough into fourths, then each batch into 24 rolls. Bake at 400⁰ for 17 minutes or until golden. Dough can be kept for several days in refrigerator and used as needed.

THE SUGAR FIX

My husband, Bron, loves this during the Thanksgiving and Christmas holidays. It makes a perfect breakfast or after dinner dessert. It's especially good when warm and spread with fresh butter. His mother gave me a base recipe and I made some adjustments to our taste and to make it more appealing to customers.

Pumpkin Bread

350°   45 minutes

½ cup peanut oil*
3 eggs
1 cup buttermilk
1 tsp. vanilla
2 cups canned pumpkin
3 ½ cups all-purpose flour
1 tsp. salt
½ tsp. ginger
½ tsp. allspice
¼ tsp. cloves
1 tsp. cinnamon
2 tsp. baking soda
3 cups sugar

Combine peanut oil, eggs, buttermilk, vanilla, and pumpkin; mix well. Sift together flour, salt, ginger, allspice, cloves, cinnamon, baking soda, and sugar. Add to pumpkin mixture; blend well. Pour into 2 prepared loaf pans. Bake for 45 minutes or until skewer comes out clean.

*Melted and cooled butter can be used in place of the peanut oil. It gives a slightly different, but wonderful flavor.

Miscellaneous Recipes

Bread machines have been a great addition to kitchen appliances. This recipe came from not having some of the ingredients listed in the book that came with my machine.

Bread Machine Bread

1 ½ lb. loaf

1 cup buttermilk
3 Tbsp. butter
1 egg
3 ½ cups all-purpose flour
2 Tbsp. sugar
1 tsp. salt
1 tsp. yeast

In microwave-proof measuring glass, warm buttermilk and butter for 1 minute on medium power. Stir, then pour into bread machine pan. Add egg, then flour, sugar, salt, and yeast. Place in bread machine and program for white bread to the degree of darkness you prefer.

Light Wheat

Substitute ½ cup whole wheat flour for ½ cup of all-purpose flour. Follow directions for wheat bread provide by manufacturer.

By using the dough only setting, you can make wonderful dinner rolls. Place equal amounts of dough in muffin pan, brush with butter, let rise to double, and then bake at 375° for 20 minutes.

THE SUGAR FIX

Sugar Fan and Flowers

Twenty-five individual blades were cut and glued together (edible gum glue) to make this black fan. It is trimmed in gold and the symbols are hand painted gold. The flowers are from a class project of Moth Orchids and Crocosmia Aura, as well as Calla Lilies. I may be crazy with my flowers, but the ribbon is real. I do draw the line at some point!

Miscellaneous Recipes

Every time I go to a cake decorating competition or other type of food art competition, people ask me how I make my flowers so thin. The secret is a very good gumpaste. Gumpaste is a type of candy clay that is rolled and formed into many things to use as edible decorations. Unlike marzipan, gumpaste dries hard and is extremely fragile.

GUMPASTE

½ lb. <u>high quality</u> fondant
2-3 tsp. tylose*
¼ - ½ tsp. gum arabic*

Knead small amounts at a time of the tylose and gum arabic into fondant. Mix until your fingers "pop" when pulled off. How much you use will depend largely on the temperature of your hands and the humidity of your area. I have very warm hands, so I use more tylose than others. Gumpaste should be stretchy. Form into a ball, then rub shortening over the entire ball. Wrap tightly in plastic wrap, twice, then store in a plastic sipper bag. Use in small amounts and keep covered.

*Tylose and gum arabic can be found at cake decorating stores. Gumpaste can be made without the gum arabic if it is not available.

THE SUGAR FIX

Hearts and Flowers

These are by far my favorite flowers. The entire piece is made with white chocolate gumpaste, the ribbon bow at the top. The roses and ribbon are pink, the carnations are white, and the blossoms are bright yellow. While it was being judged, I nearly came unglued when one of the judges touched the roses to see if they were real or silk. It took everything I had to not chew out the judge. I am happy to say that someone told both judges that they knew the flowers were made from chocolate because they knew me. I won 1st Place at the 2003 Chocolate Festival.

Miscellaneous Recipes

There are many ways to stick petals together, such as water or egg white. I prefer this particular glue. It holds quickly, without sliding, and dries invisibly. It takes a while for the tylose to absorb the water, so try making it a day ahead for best consistency.

Gum Glue

2 Tbsp. water
+/- 1/8 tsp. tylose

Mix together to form a sort of thin gelatin. I prefer a thicker glue (it will not drip off of a small paint brush), but you should experiment with what works best for you.

A judge once told me that if my flowers looked like potato chips, they were too heavy. Being obsessive-compulsive, I worked very hard to make them as thin as possible. Now when making them, I can read a business card through them.

THE SUGAR FIX

Pastillage (pronounced pah-still-ahj or pasti-ahj) is great for making very strong sugar pieces. Boxes, frames, logs, plaques, or just about anything can be made with it. It dries quickly, so it must be either kept wrapped or used VERY quickly. It also should be used immediately. It does not store well. Even when wrapped, it dries quickly. It can be kneaded with fondant to give you a little more working time, but it also increases it's drying time. Although it is strong, it will still break like glass, even to the point of sounding like a plate breaking. If you are making a large piece, it will take several days to dry. Placing it on upholstery foam will allow air to circulate to speed the process. Be sure the "pores" are small so as to not leave indentations on the back of your piece. If you need to turn it over to allow the back to dry, it must be fully supported or it will break until it has completely dried.

Pastillage

4 cups powdered sugar
1 Tbsp. gum tragacanth
+/- ¼ cup water

Stir together the powdered sugar and gum tragacanth. Add the water in small amounts, stir with a wooden spoon until crumbly. The knead until the "dough" is smooth. Wrap immediately in plastic wrap.

Miscellaneous Recipes

Sugar Doll

This doll is completely chocolate, including the flowers and head. Her face is hand painted with food coloring and the flowers on the dress are made with the
Chocolate Leather. I made this just to see if I could. I was very pleased with the results.

THE SUGAR FIX

I use this recipe to make flowers, figures, and other decorations for cakes. It tastes wonderful and stores well at room temperature and in the freezer. It is also easy to handle. After the flower or other piece cools, it can be moved without worry of damage.

CHOCOLATE LEATHER

1 cup <u>inexpensive</u> chocolate coating
1 cup marshmallow cream

Place ingredients into a microwave proof bowl, then nuke for 1 minute on high. Stir to melt chocolate. Heat in 15 second increments to finish melting chocolate. The hot marshmallow cream will continue to melt the chocolate, so do no over nuke. Allow mixture to cool enough to handle. It should look like a stringy, yucky mess. Be sure to wear an apron and work over the sink, as this is a mess job. Have a piece of plastic wrap on the counter next to the sink, then take ¼ of the mixture at a time and knead and squeeze out excess oil until it becomes tacky; set on plastic wrap. After kneading the small portions, knead all of them together to continue to work out excess oil. Wrap in plastic wrap and allow the "leather" to come to room temperature or over night. To use, cut off a small amount and knead until soft.

About The Author

Michele started decorating cakes when she decided to stay at home with kids, but needed something to do. After a few years of having a home based business, her husband talked her into opening a shop. So she opened a small bakery/restaurant in Choctaw, Oklahoma. She made delicious homemade cakes, cookies, pies, a variety of desserts, sandwiches, and soups. Michele is a perfectionist and an extremely picky eater. These factors highly influenced how she ran her business and developed her recipes. The Sugar Fix was only open for a short time due to the sudden onset of Multiple Sclerosis, but the ideas, principles, and flavors are carried on in this book.

Printed in the United States
52972LVS00006B/283-300